The Fascination with Death in Contemporary French Thought

Betty Rojtman

The Fascination with Death in Contemporary French Thought

A Longing for the Abyss

Translated by Bartholomew Begley

palgrave
macmillan

Betty Rojtman
Hebrew University of Jerusalem
Jerusalem, Israel

Translated by
Bartholomew Begley
Dublin City University
Dublin, Ireland

ISBN 978-3-030-47321-1   ISBN 978-3-030-47322-8   (eBook)
https://doi.org/10.1007/978-3-030-47322-8

© The Author(s), under exclusive licence to Springer Nature Switzerland AG 2020
This work is subject to copyright. All rights are solely and exclusively licensed by the Publisher, whether the whole or part of the material is concerned, specifically the rights of translation, reprinting, reuse of illustrations, recitation, broadcasting, reproduction on microfilms or in any other physical way, and transmission or information storage and retrieval, electronic adaptation, computer software, or by similar or dissimilar methodology now known or hereafter developed.
The use of general descriptive names, registered names, trademarks, service marks, etc. in this publication does not imply, even in the absence of a specific statement, that such names are exempt from the relevant protective laws and regulations and therefore free for general use.
The publisher, the authors and the editors are safe to assume that the advice and information in this book are believed to be true and accurate at the date of publication. Neither the publisher nor the authors or the editors give a warranty, expressed or implied, with respect to the material contained herein or for any errors or omissions that may have been made. The publisher remains neutral with regard to jurisdictional claims in published maps and institutional affiliations.

This Palgrave Macmillan imprint is published by the registered company Springer Nature Switzerland AG.
The registered company address is: Gewerbestrasse 11, 6330 Cham, Switzerland

To the memory of my parents,
who gave me life

Translator's Acknowledgments

Where possible, I have used existing English translations of the texts cited, only departing from them when necessary. These departures are marked by a translator's note in the footnotes.

Thanks to Professor Rojtman for her unstinting advice during the work on this translation.

Bartholomew Begley, Government of Ireland Postdoctoral Fellow in Philosophy, Dublin City University

CONTENTS

CHAPTER 1

Introduction

Abstract The twentieth century saw the collapse of systems and beliefs. Reading some of its preeminent theoretical works, in particular those since the period between the wars, it quickly becomes clear that this tragic sense is not just recognized or suffered, but is claimed as a privilege. How can we explain this Romanticism of unhappiness, which shadows contemporary writing? Is it only the outcome of a deathly impulse? What hidden values might it be covering?

Keywords Fascination • Tragic • Twentieth century

> 'Who does not "die" of being only a man will always be only a man.'
> —*Georges Bataille*, Inner Experience

Faced with the enigma of a life perpetually changing, unceasingly reborn and corrupted, the human mind has doubtless wanted to create for itself some stable representations, images of the heavens and of thought. And yet, between the crystal and the smoke (Atlan 1979: 5), philosophy has always swung from one pole to the other, both equally threatening for consciousness: far-reaching order on the one hand and confused proliferation on the other. If the brilliance of the unmoving, its major chords, its fullness, soon won the day, the history of ideas also shows, if more discreetly, the quiet persistence of a less assured melodics, of alteration and of

© The Author(s) 2020   1
B. Rojtman, *The Fascination with Death in Contemporary French Thought*, https://doi.org/10.1007/978-3-030-47322-8_1

turmoil.[1] Since at least the Romantic era, modern man has leaned toward the values of what is passing, of movement, of evanescence. The ideal is no longer to abstract from the ferment of Nature an intelligible unity or some celestial archetype, but rather to unveil the hidden face, the chaotic and Dionysian reserves. Today, it is these reserves, after so many centuries of a marmoreal metaphysics, which have come center stage. It is these dislocations, arising from some subterranean heritage, which are pushing thought to turn now toward the uncertain, to read the world as indeterminate.

This disintegrating approach, today commonplace, which would call into doubt all coherence and all exactitude, is nonetheless ambiguous; it has no obvious concern bar an irreparable break, a disorder for its own sake, as if the goal were now to raise to the theoretical level something more unstable and equivocal: the weariness with existence, the dissipation and ephemerality of all things. The decay to which each being is heir thus winds its way to the heart of the system, a deep-seated disequilibrium, the accident which is in fact necessity. For were it not for this logic of entropy, how could one understand why our modernity has chosen exile as its emblem? Or why the infatuation with finitude, echoed in so many contemporary works, both poetic and critical, has so long marked our aging civilization?

It is at the heart of these questions that we must place the sumptuous, stifling and 'negative' forms of twentieth-century writing. Against the seductive artifices of the whole, the mirages of the rational, they put up, in literature as in philosophy, the anarchic forces of the human tragedy: Pain, Anguish, Exile. Agents of a necessary subversion, these paradigms of loss undo identities, erode reference points and break through the barrier of meaning. Witnesses on behalf of that which in experience can no longer find its end or its close, they form the credo of a new ethics, a salvation through lack that wrenches the infinite off its base, and that wards off, by means of the void, the crush of presence.

In this primordial drama, Death plays the lead role, its disintegrating power, its eyes gouged out: anything which harrows out its pain within us, which denatures us in order to hand us over to the insubstantial. Death the bandit undoes our moorings, shakes off the chains of the concrete. There's a shackle to be broken, a trap to be escaped, into weightlessness.

---

[1] We would note here a traditional opposition which goes back to the pre-Socratics. For a study of this dichotomy, see Beaufret (2013), in particular pp. 17ff.

Since Hegel, it is by traversing precipices that man has reached the self, in the horror of one's will to look and see.

A wayfaring *for death*, then, 'as one goes forth unto death' (Levinas 1979: 34). It has given rise in passing, in the century of collapses—our century—to many a knight errant. Against the suffocation of the real, captains have risen up. Thomas Mann, Pessoa or Beckett—toward what out-of-bounds, what *no world's land*,[2] more essential than life itself?

In France, for over a century, an exquisite sense of forsakenness has imbued literature, a nobility in abandonment, something like pride. Like a passion for being, setting its face against the living. Since the period between the wars, a slew of critical texts, an entire legacy of ruptures, effusions, fluidities, has admitted its debt to the master of Jena—but on the side of nothingness, on the side of that which gives up, that can no longer form a whole or be understood.[3] On the side of the flaw, and the slippage, the shores of change and of the unquiet unanswered question, Kojève, Bataille and Blanchot, spanning the century, cast off plenitude like a worn-out suit. The shade of Heidegger, irresistibly, encroaches on modern thought.[4] A family waiving its claim, averse to what's offered, to the continuous, to material and plenteous sustenance. A refusal to be satisfied, a rejection of any fullness of light.

Whence this deviance, this initiatory collapse that sets the subject afloat, so painfully diaphanous and isolated? In our age of conquest, what to

[2] [Translator's note: in English in the text.]

[3] For Vincent Descombes, the philosophical 'first generation' of the twentieth century is that of the 'three Hs' (Hegel, Husserl, Heidegger). The seminar given by Kojève at the *École Pratique des Hautes Études*, beginning in 1933, thus marks the 'resurgence of Hegel' and the renewal of French thought (1979: 21). One generation later, the 1960s, with the dominance of the masters of suspicion, will see a reversal in attitudes: Hegel has become the enemy. And yet, in this 'inversion of the sign that marks the relationship to Hegel,' something remains unchanged: 'the reference point itself remained the same, but in the one case the concern was with drawing towards it [...] whereas in the other it was with drawing away [...]' (1979: 12).

Taking as our Ariadne's thread the fascination with death, in the sense in which Kojève approached it, our reading will seek to examine this continuity which transcends the turning points and ruptures of the century, even into its post-modern extensions.

[4] For Heidegger's identification of the essence of being with nothingness and the 'primordial gaping,' see Zarader (2006: 130–135).

relate to this strategy of renouncement, like a deadly alchemy whose secret, handed down through the ages, now finally overcomes us?[5]

Is it from the depths of Greece that this bitter discordance arises, this pose of the philosopher 'practicing to die,' as if to better escape the constraints, the tender traps, of the sensible, in order to save the essential, which denounces the perishable shell, and serenely drinks the hemlock? Is it from the *Phaedo* that this inversion of suffering springs forth, this abstinence transmuted into victory, when immortality binds itself to death, trusts itself to it, gives itself over to the trial of an infinite dying?

Or perhaps it's from an obsessive, Christian iconography—that image of Calvary in its strange tenacity, this chiaroscuro little by little sublated, which changes into resurrection and a revelation of light? Is it to the 'paradox of the crucified One' (Dastur 1996: 14), so deeply anchored in our collective memory, that we owe this melancholic longing for death, the ecstasy of passivity, which still stokes our mythic imaginary?[6]

Across history, in various guises, these anthropological structures have surreptitiously continued to exercise their magnetism. From the critique of appearances to the negation of the divine, from the praise of thought to the glorification of nothingness, they have been digging the ditch between the human and life. Reform, Cartesian humanism, Renaissance skepticism: from century to century, the 'search after truth'[7] has levied its ransom of denial and incertitude. A Pascalian eagle spreads its sorrow little by little, touches with its snowy wing the thinking subject (cf. Vigée 1960: 24–29). After Chateaubriand come Baudelaire and Mallarmé, after Byron and Jean-Paul Richter, Hofmannsthal then Rilke (cf. Vigée 1960: 71–82).

In this crepuscular collapse, one configuration remains obdurate which expresses acquiescence of consciousness in its own disappearance, a mysticism little by little laicized[8] and torn, where the conflict of man and nature

---

[5] Let me salute here the memory of Philippe Lacoue-Labarthe, whose powerful seminar on Death, held at the Paul Desmarais Center in Jerusalem in 1996, was so important for the evolution of my own thinking.

[6] It is with good reason that Georges Bataille recognizes, in this sacrificial devotion, in this duty to 'imitate in God (Jesus) the fall from grace, the agony, the moment of "non-knowledge" of the "Lama sabachthani,"' a pious prefiguration of modern negativism (1988: 47). Note that Schopenhauer had already seen in the Savior 'the symbol or personification of the negation of the will to life' (2010, t. I: § 70: 433).

[7] This is the title of a work by Nicolas Malebranche (1674–1675), the first books of which deal with the errors due to man.

[8] Georges Bataille defined the *atheistic mystic* as one who 'conscious of having to die and to disappear, would live [...] in absolute disintegration,' but would never come out of it

is secularized, showing its transhistorical force. God is dead, who called man to distance himself from the vanities of this world; no artesian well bursts forth deep in the desert. But, strangely persevering, inaccessible to these revolutions, the gesture of denial persists, which no longer brings any compensation, no longer offers any refuge as justification. As if this image of the cross, and this entrusting oneself unto death, maintained their grip, after the reasons to hold to them had disappeared. Consciousness enters the realm, until now proscribed, of the 'impossible supposition,' of an absurd godlessness, of a world immured and echoless, but that one must nonetheless love with a 'pure love,'[9] as if Silence alone held salvation within it. Claude Vigée calls this slow hollowing out of substance 'symbolist,' by which man loses all hold on the real, and takes on the enchanting pallor of an Ophelia (cf. Vigée 1960: 56–60).[10]

Thus, death becomes a path, by the distortion of concepts where one sees, as through a glass darkly, the shape of a more ancient *passion*. Death takes up an empty square, the silent region of theology. Since the start of the nineteenth century, it has taken over this task. A sooty substitute, it is the 'elective form,' the black invisibility, under which at present the 'absolute is thought'[11]: one could say of it 'what western tradition says so well of God,' that it is 'something than which it is impossible to conceive anything greater.'[12]

This rejection, then, today appears more decided, a need without end, more ravenous than any search, more savage, stripped bare and gaunt, pushing us toward the baptismal waters of the negative. The approach is no longer oblique, with the humility of hope, but goes straight to the 'radical caesura' to the 'purely and simply unthinkable thing' (Dastur 1996: 38). A haughty confrontation, without resolution, that is freely undertaken, that 'argues for "no passage beyond" death, and proposes no transcendence capable of neutralizing it' (Dastur 1996: 40).

(1997: 294 n. 6). [Translator's note: I have departed here from the translation in Bataille (1997).]

[9] Cf. Fénelon (1983), 'Sur le pur amour': 656–671. On p. 661 we find the principle of the 'impossible supposition.' Note that Schopenhauer himself said of Madame Guyon, who inspired Fénelon: 'The memory of this great and beautiful soul always fills me with awe' (2010: § 68: 411–412).

[10] Reflection on the symbol and its de-realizing power forms the fabric of Vigée's text.

[11] Cf. Jackson (1982: 117), 'Death [...] is the elective form under which Baudelaire thinks the absolute.'

[12] Françoise Dastur uses here an expression of Saint Anselm of Canterbury (1996: 3).

Hope, now adulterated, fallacious and obsolete, is not absent: it has simply become the enemy, fixed in its role of Gorgon. Standing in the face of disaster, the man of denial will 'refuse [...] to be saved' (Bataille 1988: 43). This cold insistence on no longer being tricked is expressed with a suppressed exaltation, in a sort of impassive fervor, where the noble recognize one another. For at the end of the day salvation via metaphysics is only an opium of the poor. Our generation, more demanding, enjoys the lofty peaks: it 'needs truth, not consolation' (Nancy 2002: 4), climbing with its lordly step the stony paths, in the biting and rarefied air. Its impatience is that of princes, whom nothing satisfies. Tired of so many lies, of drab responses, of tumbled-down systems.

United in one and the same abstention, some notable authors have opted for the side of the unfulfilled, of what differs, of that which breaks through encirclements—for the side of 'quietude' or disinterest, against the 'kingdom of nature' or its 'necessity' (cf. Schopenhauer 2010: § 70). Everywhere, the same attraction to Breaking, the same profusion of contingency.

Little by little, nourished by their disappointment, these knights take up residence in dispossession as their very condition, the dead end as their only path, the royal road of an inexhaustible questioning. One comes slowly to suspect a *desire for desire*, a desire for absence for its own sake, stronger than any compensations. As if the human meant the watchman's alertness, that one did not want repose, that one did not want anything that would bring to an end the direction or the movement, but only the marvelous rush, this infatuation with the abyss and white spaces.

To the concerns which are properly philosophical are added, therefore, in a manner ever more feverish, a series of lateral affects, which are decisive for the argument. It is on rereading these emblematic pages, listening, perhaps, for certain rhythms and certain accents, on the lookout for repetitions and insistences, for sudden gaps in the exposition, that one can hope to discover, under the rhetorical fabric, betrayed by that fabric, a more furtive ideology, a profound engagement of the whole person, which gives this process its coherence and its 'virtue.' Centered on the heart of the twentieth century, in the decades after the great collapse of 1870,[13]

---

[13] The defeat of 1870 and its consequences—the fall of the Empire, the loss of Alsace-Lorraine, the Paris Commune—remains a critical date in the history of ideas. It exacerbates the rejection of the Romantic idealism which had been in vogue since the middle of the nineteenth century. In literature, it nourishes the bitter lucidity of realism as well as symbolist

our reading will try to work out, within the various manifestations of the theme, the meaning of this recognizable fascination; it will investigate the scar, the subterranean values, the lure of the vertiginous.

The profound contemporary sadness shows itself, then, to be inseparable from a *jouissance* which raises a question in its own right, with its yearning for the wasteland, an obstinacy in damnation, which any reader who is any way attentive can't help but notice. It allows us to see, beyond the dismay, under the long mourning and the denunciation, still a sort of belief, an ideal without object, defended with ardor. As if one had to acknowledge, within this very resignation, all the more vast and all the more sharp from the twentieth century on, in the admission that the race is run and Atlantis lost, an essential, an extreme, point, worth all the throes of death, a sort of joy, yes, an inexplicable satisfaction, a sort of vehemence risen from the depths.

Without regard for what has been achieved up to now, the hero of modernity sees himself above all as a citizen of the foreign, stateless, torn free of all moorings. He throws himself upon an ocean of insatiable expectations, '[which] no journey, no change of climate or scenery can satisfy' (Levinas 1979: 33). Like the vagabond pilgrim who never gives up his fever, never at ease, hunting down in his impatience some unseen beyond. Levinas will call this desire of the absolutely other 'metaphysical,' fed on separation and hunger, wearing itself out transgressing limits or anything which weighs on us and fixes us, in every corner of the tangible. In a spellbound torment, wherever, far from the possible, man aims for *that which is not*. In order, perhaps, not to be contented, to quench one's thirst only with thirst, in an ever-growing intoxication, to not reach a goal, drifting among enchanted reefs, toward the absolutely irreparable.

For these unquiet pursuits the unthinkable suffices, something in the soul that swoons at the perspective of the fall, that consents to it and is more completely fulfilled by it than by any promise, than by any joy too strait for its measure, something in the soul which only the mad excess of perdition can soothe. We must ask what is 'added' to the aporias of former times by this difficult and more recent adventure, which undoes us quite. Whence at heart this enthusiasm, in the name of what post-modern 'Romanticism,' this redemptive conviction, from what imprescriptible

disenchantment, complementary crystallizations of the 'negation of the will to life.' It is also at this period that Schopenhauer's philosophy penetrates European sensibility and marks it with its pessimism (cf. Schopenhauer 2010: § 68).

truth, from what utopia in devastation, which places the human at the source of the infinite, and comes to reap true life at the lips of Thanatos? In this rising wind, should we see just a perversion of our civilizing *élan*, in this gaiety of the shipwrecked, a death drive, in the Freudian sense of discontent, a return of the sting, working silently for the disintegration of the living (cf. Freud 1930/1961: 97)? Whence this inaptitude for light, which denounces the Eros of any will, in the name of what fragility, of what peace within the hurt, after wrestling with the Angel? 'Irrecuperable,' like the young Hugo of Sartre's 'Dirty Hands,' the spirit of our times gives itself over to no project, disengages from belief with a jolt.[14]

This detachment certainly goes beyond just the wish for exorcism, the aesthetic claims, the indulgence of the 'virtues of unhappiness' (Nancy 2002: 4). Behind the regressive 'passion,' one must sense something like a different stature of man, another meaning to his destiny, when he has lost everything, when he is nothing more than a wreckage. One must sense, in the heavens by which he steers his frail barque, a fixed star that shines still, with its backward light, even though the redemption it invokes be sterile, corrupting and truncated.

Any response can only come from negation itself, woven of this weight-lessness, this 'absolute dissolution' which the tumult of death brings with it. Only anguish can reveal the expatriation consubstantial with man, his 'basic strangeness'; only it can render him unto his native precariousness, his anarchic turmoil, like the droplets in a cloud, his existence as fleeting as the touch of silk on skin, that no theory can capture: it is only at this cost, in 'this lightness that is more than human' where 'all ground is lacking,' in abdication and emptiness, that the 'I' wins its aura, that it reaches its culmination, the essential metamorphosis through which its 'existence as burden,' at last undone, 'is transformed into grace' (Dastur 1996: 84).

Negative passion thus offers itself as the titanic, insatiable, form of human need, and one of the most heroic. But it has its blinkers and its

---

[14] Doubtless, great voices have not been lacking—first and foremost that of Ricœur—to defend, in our troubled era, the duty to affirm life. But this 'ethic of the desire to be' (cf. Ricœur 1974: 452) perhaps less refutes the presuppositions of negative philosophy than it questions its conclusions. The very *élan* of life seems to be 'tied to' a constitutive 'absence of being' (cf. Ricœur 2009/1960: 153). See also Revault d'Allonnes (2006) and Olivier Abel (2007: 14): '"Only the grieving will be consoled" writes Ricœur in the notes for the structure of his manuscript [...] melancholy is not something from which one must at all costs be delivered, for it is part of our condition.'

misunderstandings which burden the advance of our civilization with an exorbitant, tragically lavish price.

This perplexity will lead us, in the end, to attempt some changes of perspective, to explore other models of reflection, from parallel cultures, in particular that of the Hebrew Kabbalah—which, as we know, from the Renaissance on, provided a subterranean inspiration to our philosophy. Its off-center point of view, neither radically foreign nor completely the same, posits at its foundation a continual vibration of being, a circulation of energy, which evades all systematization. In opposition to a truth that is finished and gathered into its own sphere, the Kabbalah helps us to think an unstable, dynamic form of perfection, represented by the infinite of the straight line.[15] More generally speaking, the Judaic tradition bases its analysis of the human experience on the indeterminable and the fleeting. Through its differential approach and its versatile laws, it inscribes the uncertain even with the theological—and can, by virtue of this, help to change, by enriching them, our own automatic cultural reflexes.

So that a path opens that does not undo reference points, that does not impose renunciation—but that, on the contrary, surges toward the future, beyond petrifying ecstasy, and at least allows one to live, without returning to that which once was.

So that from this very debris, on this burned heath where what seems clear is lost, and its paths are a jumble—like, in old graveyards, the tombstones knocked by the storm—that from this defeat and this forgetfulness, something else can arise. A response that would no longer be only resistance or reinvention, a positing of finitude—but an ontology of dispersion, a plenitude of shards and sparks, that would rediscover by that means its path of endurance. It would no longer erect as a dogma the permanence of forms, would no longer repeat the patterns of identity—but rather melt into the unnumberable, following 'the undulations of the real' (Bergson 1946: 34). A metaphysics of the margin, missing out on totality, which would speak the absolute in terms of haze and approximation. Which would speak the incalculable, the shimmer of the ambiguous, in the very heart of the One. In tune with a physics of particles, which would proclaim fluctuation, ratifying the indeterminate, conflating the Idea and becoming. A rhythm, a breath, made of inadequacies and lapses, a lacunary and throbbing truth—but which would elevate itself, by this very

---

[15] Cf. Chap. 7 of this book: 'The Fluidity of Being: The Kabbalah.'

collapse, this vertigo, to the oxymoronic, scandalous and re-enlivening title of 'metaphysics of life' (Bergson 1946: 35).

BIBLIOGRAPHY

Abel, Olivier. 2007. *Paul Ricœur: Vivant jusqu'à la mort.* Paris: Seuil.
Atlan, Henri. 1979. *Entre le cristal et la fumée: Essai sur l'organisation du vivant.* Paris: Seuil.
Bataille, Georges. 1988. *Inner Experience.* Trans. L.A. Boldt. New York: SUNY Press.
———. 1997. Hegel, Death and Sacrifice. Trans. J. Strauss. In *The Bataille Reader*, ed. F. Botting and S. Wilson, 279–295. London: Blackwell.
Beaufret, Jean. 2013. *Parménide, le Poème.* Paris: Presses Universitaires de France.
Bergson, Henri. 1946. *The Creative Mind.* Trans. M.L. Andison. New York: Philosophical Library.
Dastur, Françoise. 1996. *Death: An Essay on Finitude.* Trans. J. Llewelyn. London and Atlantic Highlands, NJ: Athlone.
Descombes, Vincent. 1979. *Le Même et l'Autre: quarante-cinq ans de philosophie française (1933–1978).* Paris: Minuit.
Fénelon, François. 1983. Lettres et Opuscules spirituels XXIII. In *Œuvres I*, ed. Jacques Le Brun. Paris: Gallimard.
Freud, Sigmund. 1930/1961. *Civilization and its Discontents* Trans. J. Riviere. London: Hogarth Press.
Jackson, John E. 1982. *La Mort Baudelaire: Essai sur les Fleurs du Mal.* Neuchâtel: La Baconnière.
Levinas, Emmanuel. 1979. *Totality and Infinity: An Essay on Exteriority.* Trans. A. Lingis. The Hague: Martinus Nijhoff.
Nancy, Jean-Luc. 2002. *Hegel: The Restlessness of the Negative.* Trans. J. Smith and S. Miller. Minneapolis: University of Minnesota Press.
Revault d'Allonnes, Myriam. 2006. *Cet Éros par quoi nous sommes dans l'Être.* Esprit 3: 276–289.
Ricœur, Paul. 1974. *Conflict of Interpretations.* Ed. D. Ihde. Northwestern University Press.
Schopenhauer, Arthur. 2010. *The World as Will and Representation.* Trans. and ed. J. Norman et al. Cambridge: Cambridge University Press.
Vigée, Claude. 1960. *Les Artistes de la faim.* Paris: Calmann-Lévy.
Zarader, Marlène. 2006. *The Unthought Debt: Heidegger and the Hebraic Heritage.* Trans. B. Bergo. Stanford: Stanford University Press.

CHAPTER 2

Human Death: *Alexandre Kojève*

Abstract Our analysis takes as its starting point the seminar 'Introduction to *The Phenomenology of Spirit*,' which Kojève taught in Paris in the 1930s and which left its mark on generations of intellectuals. In his presentation, Kojève deconstructs the image of a 'monist' Hegel and draws attention to the profoundly dualist sense of his thought. As consciousness-subject, man opposes the world that surrounds him and also opposes his own nature as living being. This confrontation with death, that is, the assumption of his finitude, becomes the mark of man's grandeur and of his liberty.

Keywords Finitude • Animal/human • Liberty • Negation • Thomas Hobbes

With the arrival in Paris of Alexandre Kojève, in the early 1930s, a whole new intellectual climate took hold in France. The seminar 'Introduction to *The Phenomenology of Spirit*,' which Kojève taught every week at the *École Pratique des Hautes Études*, attracted the finest minds of the age and marks a key moment in the history of French philosophy[1]; long afterward, it would continue to hold a strange attraction for generations of thinkers

---

[1] The list of those who attended varies from one study to another. Most often mentioned are Raymond Queneau, Georges Bataille, Michel Leiris, Roger Caillois, Maurice Merleau-Ponty, Raymond Aron, Henry Corbin, Jean Hyppolite, Eric Weil, Jacques Lacan, Gaston Fessard, Pierre Klossowski and Alexandre Koyré.

© The Author(s) 2020
B. Rojtman, *The Fascination with Death in Contemporary French Thought*, https://doi.org/10.1007/978-3-030-47322-8_2

and writers. Kojève's 'Hegel' quickly becomes the internal reference, 'the origin of everything new and original in philosophy' (Filoni 2010: 18).[2] His feverish exposition is testament to the anthropological preoccupations of the time, placing man, the sense of man as consciousness and as destiny, at the heart of his reflection.[3]

In fact, Kojève's interpretation, resolutely tendentious and not a little manipulative,[4] directly poses the existential question: What is it to live? What is left of man when one has taken everything from him? This recurring question became part of the Zeitgeist and would become all the more acute in the decades to come. Its postulates and its truths, though shaken little by little by more 'suspicious' points of view,[5] would continue nonetheless, quietly but insistently, to mark French intellectual activity.

In Kojève's reformulation, Hegel is not the thinker of the System, the great apostle of totality who denounces modern sensibility. The aspect Kojève foregrounds is not that of an Absolute to be revealed, which would amount in the end to a single and self-contained Knowledge, but rather, at the very heart of substance, an unceasing corrosion, an obstinate will to destroy, growing out of human pain. In opposition to the 'monist' vision of Hegel, 'which seemed to [him] an error' (Jarczyk and Labarrière 1996: 64),[6] Kojève thus defends a dialectic *dualism*, that is, the idea of an irreparable fracture between man and world, between man's negating action

---

[2] 'The seminar which Kojève held at the *École Pratique des Hautes Études*, at 5.30 pm every Monday to start, then every Friday, between 1933 and 1939, is part of the cultural memory of the time. Legend would have any number of the future intellectuals of the post-war era arriving at their fundamental philosophical views there, finding their inspiration there' (Hollier 1995: 61).

[3] [Translator's note: Kojève's seminar (Kojève 1997) has not been translated into English in its entirety. Parts of it are translated in Kojève (1969), other parts in Kojève (1973).]

[4] 'It was relatively unimportant to me to know what Hegel himself wanted to say in his book; I offered a phenomenological anthropology course using Hegelian texts.' Letter from Kojève to Tran Duc Thao, dated October 7, 1948 (Jarczyk and Labarrière 1996: 64).

[5] Derrida sees in the teaching of Kojève one of the sources of the generalized anthropologism and humanism characteristic of the post-war period: '[...] humanism or anthropologism, during this period, was a common ground of Christian or atheist existentialisms, of the philosophy of values (spiritualist or not), of personalisms of the right or the left, of Marxism in the classical style. [...] This profound concordance was authorized, in its philosophical expression, by the *anthropologist* readings of Hegel [...], of Marx [...], of Husserl [...], of Heidegger, whose projects for a philosophical anthropology or an existential analytic only were known or retained' (Derrida 1982: 116–117, italics in the text).

[6] See also, on this question of Hegel's ontological monism, the important note by Kojève (1997: 485–486).

and the immobility of nature, always 'identical to itself': 'if substance, conceived of as [...] static-[and]-given-being [...] has identity [with itself] as its ontological grounding, the Subject of the Discourse [...] that is, Man, has negativity as its ultimate basis' (Auffret 1990: 344 and Kojève 1973: 116, our ellipses, square brackets in text).

The consciousness-subject, whose history Hegel retraces, refuses any determination which would entrance it. It cannot be objectified, and constitutes itself in violence, tearing itself away from the earthly dross which weighs it down. By an active undermining, a continual agitation, it frees itself of all substrate and achieves its humanity, confirming thereby its pre-eminence, its marvelous non-coincidence with everything that *is*.

Hegel thus marks a turning point, the moment of rupture, with no return, from the classic pagan conception, which saw in the anthropos 'a purely natural being' 'absolutely determined by the natural place (*topos*) that he occupies [...] in the midst of the [...] Cosmos' (Kojève 1973: 120). Contrary to Greek man, who was at one with the given, the Hegelian dialectic projects an image of solitude: a weird plant brought back from distant places, strangely singular in this blind world. Kojève's Subject shows himself yet more openly heterogeneous, incommensurable with brute matter.[7] 'Even while living in Nature, he does not submit to its laws' (1973: 120). He places himself counter to the real, as supernatural and as alterity.

This obligatory divorce extends to all worlds. Utopian, metaphysical or real, encountered or reconstructed, their point in common is that they reflect the same rigid framework, are similarly enclosed in the irrevocable. To defend themselves from the ephemeral, no doubt, to preserve an inalterable order, Greek philosophy, then Christian theology, had to transpose into being the values of 'reason' peculiar to cosmic determinism. The spiritual world thus offers the same invariability, the same asphyxiating perfection, as the terrestrial law of phenomena:

> [For Judeo-Christians] man *really* transcends the natural world in this sense, that he lives also in a *transcendent* world (and not only in a [...] world that is *immanent* to Nature). [...] Now this world does not depend on man: it is *given* to him once and for all, being 'prior' and essentially immutable in itself. (1973: 121–122, italics in the text)

---

[7] This powerful dichotomy seems to render less flexible the Hegelian back and forth and ambiguity as regards the formation of the phenomenological Subject, caught between interiority and exteriority (cf. Butler 1987: Chap. 1. pp. 17–60).

One can see, by the return of certain terms, the parallel established between the weight of concrete causalities and the closure of the transcendent universe: the superior world of immortality, icon of the tangible (that is to say, of the natural world), the '*natural place*' (1973: 122, our italics) of man after his death, is also 'given,' no less heavy and fixed than is the inert, no less impassive and perpetual. Being only the solidified reflection of material snares, the superior, transcendent world arouses the same suspicions, inspires the same distrust. Nature, even if under the species of God, continues its work of oppression and constraint:

> By force of the logic of things, Christian thought had to *subordinate* immortal man to its eternal infinite transcendent God. It had to *give up human freedom*, and therefore the true historicity and individuality of man. (1973: 122, our italics)[8]

To defend the privilege of the human would therefore be, above all, to escape the yoke of plenitude which condemns him to the eternal. If living imposes first a submission to Nature, through the Negative man frees himself of all coercion; he dodges his way out of the web of predestination. Borne by his need to be an exception, by his belief in his baroque grandeur, he entrusts himself to the nothingness through which all begins. Dialectic, from this point of view, represents only the methodological envelope of a refusal to merge, to be submerged, of an atavistic retreat before the Completed.

Throughout his life, Kojève was torn by the question of determinism, of a possible break in the chain of necessity. If, very early, he had a connoisseur's interest in the theory of quanta, it was especially because it opens a decisive caesura in the causal field; breaking with the homogeneity of classical physics, it exposes science to ideas of incertitude, chance and disorder—in other words, to that which is the basis of individual existence, and the foundation of its liberty. The movement from a philosophy of substance to a thought of the Subject aims primarily, no doubt, at giving back

[8] One encounters this same transposition and this same note of refusal with regard to other anthropological values brought into question (historicity and individuality): 'But being God, [Christ] can be nothing other than the one and unique Being who thinks himself while remaining eternally identical to himself' (1973: 122).

to the person his human face: confronted with the imperturbable universe, which rolls out its cycles eternally, man is first of all a 'Person' (1973: 120), not a thing, but *someone*. Contrary to the law of the species, he is a singular consciousness and, as such, evades capture (cf. 1973: 121).

Dialectic, in Kojève's mind, will help achieve this change: denying the given, it guarantees the autonomy of the consciousness and gives it back its unconditional plasticity. By its power of negation, dialectic removes the Subject from this petrification, from this fixation in Being which he risks being mired in. It saves the Subject from the immutable law of Nature, which Kojève here represents as conventional and frozen. Contrary to astral revolutions, which are just blind circlings, man is a historical and free individual (cf. Kojève 1997: 121): in other words, his story can be told and he has a becoming. 'Dominated in his very being by Negativity,' he escapes the given, to make of himself 'Action,' 'the Act-of-positing-itself or of creating itself' (Kojève 1973: 116). He gives the lie to matter and its crystals to espouse this dynamic *élan*, always unresolved, which hounds him—a virtuality in waiting, never equal to himself, or to his own present. Entirely 'project' or 'goal' (1973: 118), he *tends toward*, always open to a future non-place, far from the Hegelian dream of the reconquered totality. He lives in suspense, 'in function of the future,' and realizes himself 'as a work' (1973: 118) in the unforeseen of time. Pure innovation, pure meta-morphosis, by renunciation man wins his evanescent reality, in the floating sweetness of existing.

This *ecstasy* is underpinned by a poetic of Desire, on which topic Kojève's seminar opens. It is the starting point of a resistance, of an anar-chic and jealous outburst, which is at the basis of the existential protesta-tion. Desire in effect is the principle motor of this vast process of differentiation, of the establishment of the Person, through which begins the Hegelian dialectic. No longer only a reflex of dissociation, of negating annihilation, but the winning of autonomy, the revealing of self to self in a freedom 'with nothing [...] which it depends on or on which it is based' (Kant 1996, AK 4: 425), a freedom fearful only in its solitude.

Desire is this search for an elsewhere, for a crack of infinity in the anon-ymous block. In the face of sealed reality, it becomes a drill, 'a *hole* in Space' (Kojève 1997: 368, our italics), signifying only that it is not, pas-sionately opening a breach everywhere, looking for an 'outside' (cf. Filoni 2010: 215). A*nywhere out of the world* (to cite Baudelaire): Kojève shows with a shudder how the ego never grows calm, meeting everywhere the muddy mass, the aggregate of things, as it seeks the cleft and flight, in a de-realization which can only come to it from itself, from its starved hurry, from its instinct for pillage. This 'hatred of vegetation' (again to cite Baudelaire's *'petit poème'*) exiles the ego in perpetuity and leaves it only its own emptiness as sole resource:

> For there to be Self-Consciousness, Desire must therefore be directed toward a non-natural object, toward something that goes beyond the given reality. Now, *the only thing* that goes beyond the given reality is *Desire itself.* (Kojève 1969: 12, our italics)

Desire of desire: this ravening Nietzschean phrase (*'O Begierde nach Begehren!'*: Nietzsche 1969, Section 2 'The Night Song'), which Lacan places as epigraph to the eternal wandering, already for Kojève has its charge of tragic splendor. It communicates the unrelenting burning of dissatisfaction, the exasperation with that which is, the heaving with impatience, a craving for absence, which will remain fundamental in all its future expressions:

> Desire, being the revelation of an emptiness, the presence of the absence of a reality, is something *essentially different* from the desired thing, *something other than a thing*, than a static and given real being. (Kojève 1969: 5, our italics)

Desire is always bitter and hollow and knows only the abyss. It is vacancy itself, as defined by this subtraction; it is the means and sign of a transcendence from within, of a 'no in the yes' (Koyré 1971: 161–162, cited in Filoni 2010: 234) which lets one touch absence within plenitude. It is the private chasm, the continual wound which cuts into the opacity of the world.

For years, Kojève tried to develop his own philosophy, based on a theory of the inexistent—something which, without being pure nothingness, would nonetheless be perceived as an inverted, paradoxical presence, as the evidence of a 'not given' (cf. Kojève 1998: 137, and Filoni 2010: 216), a sort of 'positive' experience of negation, an actuality of non-being, a tissue of shadows.

This 'path toward nothing' (Filoni 2010: 215) is evident from the opening moments of Kojève's seminar: the negating action is not restricted to ends of survival alone, to an orgy of consumption; no, rather, the essential rupture that Desire marks should be understood as a distraction at the heart of the everyday, a shout in the night which reveals the silence. In the tension where his humanity is formed, the consciousness comes quickly to confuse himself with the tear itself, with his own effort of abstraction. By a transfer which Kojève uses and radicalizes, this negativity turns against itself and is poisoned by its own dart. If the creative act arises from a nihilation, the Subject is dissolved 'in its own being,' as an essential abolition. He is at once agent and object, intrinsically reduced to this pure separating power, no longer the repercussion of an 'absolute power,' but 'this power itself,' the cutting edge of the knife, which he embodies in his perishable being (Kojève 1973: 131).

One thus understands that the thrust of Desire, drawn little by little into the Heideggerian sphere of influence, takes a sinister turn. One with his scythe, with his negating scything, Kojève's man becomes no more than 'a death' (1973: 132); he is 'the death that lives a human life' (1973: 134). This powerful image, which expresses the awakening of consciousness to itself, reveals at the same time its sinister side. Kojève will choose to bring it back to its theological premises, the better to exploit its austere crucifixional sense. The dialectic dualism, in effect, which would take man from nature, has its origin for him in Christian doctrine: the first divorce between object and subject is within the person, inscribed into the irreconcilable conflict between soul and body.[9] This is the real conflict, the continual defeat, through which nothingness bites at the flesh:

> Nature is a 'sin' in Man and for Man: He can and must *oppose* himself to it and *negate* it in himself. (1973: 120, in italics in the text)

So it is no longer a question of only celebrating human dignity in freeing it of its chains. The great Augustinian tradition makes this freedom part of a more bitter struggle, where the entire horizon is suffering. The war is brought within, necessarily pitiless and bloody. More than contesting the natural world *around* him, man splits off from himself, from the organic machine which enables him to exist, but which he *is not*. Negation becomes a disposition to self-destruct, to contest, in man himself, the biological law, the material order that he feels as an upsurge of nausea. But consciousness can do nothing without the soma 'that serves him as

---

[9] Compare this rejection of the body with the dualism of Plato's *Phaedo*, Chaps. X–XI: 65c–67a.

support' (1973: 130): this desire for the annihilation of the beast, in ourselves, is strictly sacrificial.

The description of this admirable, suicidal movement forms the epigraph to the book's first chapter:

> For Man to really be human, for him to differ essentially and really from the animal, his human Desire must effectively win out in him over his animal Desire. For [...] *the supreme value for the animal is its animal life.* Human Desire *must therefore win out over this desire for conservation.* (Kojève 1997: 14, our italics)

The metamorphosis of the biological being into a human being, which attests to his 'miraculous' 'specificity' (1973: 131), therefore has *finitude* as its key. It is the fundamental equation, against which consciousness measures itself, to which it is called.

To arrive at himself, in the full assumption of his singularity, Man must above all *learn to die.* Engendered by death, he must 'support death and maintain [himself] in it' (1973: 132) and through it win his privilege.

This high point remains troubling. Born of the causalist pressure, hasn't this sedition through death lost its way *en route*? Hasn't it stopped serving the disparity and the salvation of the human, to surreptitiously claim pride of place for itself, and concentrate on itself the shining lights of adoration?

Alexandre Kojève seems, at first, to want to shake off the hold of this spell, to distance himself from an exclusively death-bound reading of the Hegelian Word.[10] This is the sense of his criticism of Heidegger, arguing that he has denatured the Negative:

> Heidegger has taken up again the Hegelian themes of death, but he neglects the complementary themes concerning Struggle and Labor; thus his philosophy does not succeed in rendering an account of History.[11] (1973: 156 n. 9)

---

[10] 'No, the Hegelian Sage stays firmly with his feet on the ground. His very Science has no meaning and becomes empty verbiage if it is detached from Sensation and from Desire [...] One must take into account and justify the fact that he must eat and drink in order to write the Book of Science [...] the Sage cannot deny the tangible Real in himself and outside of himself' (Kojève 1997: 425).

[11] Inversely, Kojève criticizes Marx for having neglected the theme of death and that of bloody Revolution.

Contra this mutilation, Kojève for his part will try to underline the leading role played by anguish, its active and resistant potential, firstly as a sense of an escape, a possible parry to man's distress before inert minerality. More than do Struggle and Labor, the challenge of death constitutes the most certain break from mute substance, from the inexorability of calculated realities. Death, which breaks cycles, undoes the constancy of astral revolutions. Voluntarily accepted by the individual, it becomes an event *against nature*; arbitrary and chosen,[12] it leads beyond, overcomes itself toward the human, within a world that is impersonal and constraining. In this reading, annihilation is only the tool, the instrument of a sovereignty which completes man, at the end of a bumpy road. In keeping with the spirit of Hegel, it is made to preserve: it ensures the transmutation of the given and raises it up to that form of otherness that is human consciousness.

But at a deeper level, from the moment that it is intentional, the Subject's death belongs to him. It comes under no law; it is his, absolute and without appeal to any higher authority. From that moment, it assumes this majestic ascendant, its purple luster of allegory. 'Understood as an "immanent" or "autonomous" end' (1973: 135), death is there to proclaim man's ontological independence, his insubordination and his grandeur.

In the writings of the young Hegel, the desire for death, for a 'violent and free' death, marks the pinnacle of this immunity. At the limit of human life, at the instant of losing that life, 'the Subject demonstrates itself as free [...] absolutely raised above all constraint' (Hegel 1979, cited in Kojève 1973: 139). He 'can, absolutely, make abstraction of everything, abandon everything; [he] cannot be made dependent, [he cannot] be held (*gehalten*) by anything' (Hegel 1913, cited in Kojève 1973: 140). One can understand the intoxicating gaiety of this superior *caprice*,[13] this unbounded floating, which sees us 'escape the confinement of *no matter what* given condition of existence'[14] (1973: 140, in italics in the text).

---

[12] 'Unlike Heidegger, Hegel affirms that it is not the anguish of the passive contemplation of the approach of one's biological end, but only the anguish in and through the fight to the death [...]—that it is only death revealed in and through the negating struggle that has [...] human value' (Kojève 1993: 39).

[13] The expression is Hegel's (cited in Kojève 1973: 140).

[14] This is what Hegel said so forcefully in his *System of Ethical Life*, in 1802: 'through the faculty (*Fahigkeit*) of death the Subject demonstrates (*erweist*) itself as free and as absolutely raised above all constraint (*Zwang*)' (cited in Kojève 1973: 139).

In this dream and this excess, the question of determinism finds its resolution: the urge toward death had as its real object only to lead one to some imprescriptible lightness, far beyond natural conditionings; it prepares the infinite detachment of consciousness, and this status of impudent and mortal god, indifferent to the crush of matter. The draw toward suicide includes therefore a hope of disorder, a disruptive wish, that breaks the vise of reflexive functionings:

> In the extreme case, [Man] risks his life and has killed himself without a valid biological reason. (Kojève 1973: 137, our italics)

It is not only external causality, mechanical or biological, that is here called into question, but organicity as such, its mathematically verifiable effect. We can glimpse a sort of theoretical indulgence for this posture of radical *indetermination*, as if, taken to its extreme, the libertarian revolt seems to reanimate the 'quantic' themes of unpredictability and contingence, which are so close to contemporary concerns.

This desire for chaos supports, at a deeper level, an ethic of the unconditioned, which appears as its hidden motivation. The *for no reason* of 'deconstruction' introduces in fact a new order of values, a complex of symbols and of representations, ruled by disinterestedness. This moral of aimlessness goes beyond the sole concern for autonomy and extraterritoriality: it accords perfectly with man's lofty and royal nature, in his disdain for any plebeian condition. His haughty demands, like something come down from an age of castles and courtliness, recall ancient glories, forgotten identities, which seem to link with the heroic tradition and chivalries of yesteryear:

> To be sure, the idea of death does not add to the *well-being* of man; it does not make him *happy*, and procures no *pleasure* for him, nor any joy. But it is unique in being able to *satisfy his pride*. (Kojève 1973: 135, in italics in the text)

This 'pride' is the prerogative of the prince, freed from the natural yoke and liberated from all need. The plea for the grandeur of man, his freedom, his magnificence, turn out to be overlaid, as by a double exposure, by an archaic imagery, a huzzah of lances and shouted acclamations, which takes it out of the pure 'existential' realm and into a sociology of the passions.

We should recall that, from its introductory chapter, Kojève's seminar based the advent of consciousness on the *ego instincts*. Human Desire, which we thought so restless, so haunted by nothingness, finally comes to ground on its own reflection:

> Now, to desire a Desire is to want *to substitute oneself for the value desired* by this Desire. [...] Therefore, to desire the Desire of another is in the final analysis to desire *that the value that I am* or that I 'represent' *be the value desired by the other.* I want him to *'recognize' my value* as his value, I want him to 'recognize' me as an autonomous value. (Kojève 1969: 7, our italics)

The eagerness to transcend all gravity seems to have fallen away from its initial intention, to have fallen back into the coarse satisfactions of self-esteem. Substituting itself for Nothingness, the ego offers itself as the privileged object of the other's desire; the Ego now occupies the empty place, where were felt the pangs of the immaterial hunger of every consciousness. In this ego-centric logic, the fight to the death with the rival becomes a struggle 'for pure prestige' (1969: 7), where each one seeks to be 'recognized' and to 'impose itself on the other as the supreme value' (1969: 7). We are no longer very far from a simple feudal ethics, an 'idle and warlike'[15] ideal where the lord must only prove his bravery, that he has that 'heroic virtue' which the humanism of Hobbes applauded.[16]

Kojève's presentation here agrees, at least partially, with the English philosopher's model, which no doubt inspired Hegel.[17] Indeed, according to Hobbes, the violence of the individual surpasses the pure instinct of conservation or of enjoyment. The motive for war, for every war, as confrontation and as risk, is profoundly narcissistic:

---

[15] Kojève cites the *System of Ethical Life*, where Hegel defines the 'authentically human' life of the nobility by its character as 'idle' and 'essentially [a] warrior [class]'—a conception which he will later reject (cf. Kojève 1973: 144). The dialectic of the master and slave does, however, have some elements congruent with this ideology.

[16] Cf. Thomas Hobbes, *English Works*, Vol. 8: vi (a translation of Thucydides' *History of the Grecian War*), cited by Strauss (1952: 85 n. 1). In Hobbes' mind, virtue as 'honor' prevails over virtue understood as 'honesty.'

[17] In his essay on Hobbes, first published in 1936, Leo Strauss recalls the Hobbesian origin of the dialectic of the master and the slave. He mentions in a note a project to undertake, together with 'M. Alexandre Kojevnikoff,' a detailed investigation of the connection between Hegel and Hobbes (Strauss 1952: 58 n. 1).

Also because there be some, that taking pleasure in contemplating their own power in the acts of conquest, *which they pursue farther than their security requires.* [...] Again [...] every man looketh that his companion should value him, at the same rate he sets upon himself: and upon all signs of contempt [...] naturally endeavours, as far as he dares [...] to extort a greater value from his contemners. (Hobbes 1994, Part I: Chap. 13 §§4–5: 75–76, our italics)

This theme of 'competition' and of 'glory' will be underlined by Leo Strauss in his commentary.[18] The master's haughtiness, he tells us, his physical and moral valor, are born, in Hobbes, from a 'natural appetite' for domination, from an interest in appearance, which is aristocratic concern for oneself:

All passions and all forms of madness are modifications of conceit or of a sense of inferiority, [...] of the striving after precedence and recognition of that precedence. According to Hobbes's view, the motive of this striving is man's wish to take pleasure in himself by considering his own superiority, his own recognized superiority, i.e. vanity. (Strauss 1952: 12)

This vain pleasure, with its panoply of egoist fevers—ambition, pride and the passion for fame—marks for Hobbes 'the characteristic difference between man and animal' (Strauss 1952: 11). But this distinctive trait of the human,[19] so precious, so feverishly sought after, isn't it the same one that Kojève had seen in the desire for recognition, in the sweaty jousting of the knights? This brutal and courtly vision, made up of arrogance, temerity and *virtus*, doesn't it match Kojève's own discourse, his own avowal of elitism, where the intoxication of courage is mixed with disdain, where the ideal is molded from an excessive insolence?

What gives Kojève's writing its enchanting power, its influence over later generations, goes beyond the juvenile and fantastic, however. Its magic comes, in fact, from a redistribution of the issues. Considering more closely the intersection of the various themes, one sees in fact that, in the

---

[18] Strauss shows us Hobbes's evolution. The order of values which predominated during the 'humanist' period (particularly in the *Elements of Law* and *De Cive*), slowly inverts, most clearly from the *Leviathan* on. 'Heroic virtue' and 'honor' give way to 'magnanimity,' to 'justice' and the denunciation of pride. In the final analysis, it is the *fear of death* which is at the basis of ethics (cf. Strauss 1952: Chap. IV).

[19] Hobbes offers a list of determining factors (Hobbes 1994, Part II: Chap. 17 §2: 106).

light provided by Kojève, a new constellation takes shape. Something has changed. The fantasy of domination, which was constitutive of the Hobbesian analysis, supported, in that view, primarily the lust for life: the exacerbated ego '[claimed] his superiority' (cf. Strauss 1952: 20) as a matter of course, spreading everywhere its vitalist tumult and sprawling demands. But the English moralist is careful to clearly distinguish between those bellicose and irrational drives, *which tend toward pleasure*,[20] and the fear of death, which rather cools the *élan*.[21] After the dream of an 'ever-greater triumph over others' (Strauss 1952: 18) comes the bitter awakening of reason: it puts a check on the ego's aggressiveness, revealing to it more concretely the horror of the end, which is '*The chiefest of natural evils*.'[22] The battle with the other was authentically one of conquest: it sought the laurels of victory. It is only gradually that this desire turns to murder, that hate prevails, which carries the reason, despite itself, to the point of disaster.[23]

This obsession with the regard of the other, with his submission, with his servility, effectively reappears, in almost identical form, in the Kojévian imagery, but its role is reversed. The distribution of energies is no longer the same: *death has changed sides*. Its role is no longer to temper, but rather it polarizes the aristocratic turbulences; far from restraining the vehemence of the ego, it spurs and aggrandizes it. Thus, ostentation, arrogance, the frenzy for supremacy, *no longer oppose* the specter of Death as drives toward life; they yield to its fascination. Transgressing classifications, pride comes to serve the supreme ill; the fabulous duel is no longer that of master and slave, but that of Man and his Death. As if hypnotized by a superior Holy Grail, the Arthurian quest turns away from its courtly goals, though keeping the external forms. The passion for recognition,

---

[20] Cf. Strauss (1952: 18): 'For if man's natural appetite is vanity, this means that man by nature strives to surpass all his fellows and to have his superiority recognized by all others, in order that he may take pleasure in himself.'

[21] Cf. Hobbes (1949: Chap. 1 , §2): 'All the mind's pleasure is either glory...or refers to glory in the end; [...] All society therefore is either for gain, or for glory. [...] But no society can be great, or lasting, which begins from vain glory...I hope nobody will doubt but that men would much more greedily be carried by nature, if all fear were removed, to obtain dominion, than to gain society.'

[22] Hobbes (1949: Chap 1, §7). Also in Chap. 1, §7: 'It is therefore neither absurd, nor reprehensible, neither against the dictates of true reason, for a man to use all his endeavours to preserve and defend his body and the members thereof from death and sorrows.'

[23] Cf. Hobbes (2008), Part 1 'Human nature': Chap. IX, § 6: 'To kill is the aim of them that hate, to rid themselves of fear; revenge aimeth at triumph, which over the dead is not.'

with its panoply of radiant values, its suzerain seductiveness, now takes on exclusively the experience of anguish and the struggle with the Angel.

We are far now from the shimmering boastfulness of the ego. The memory of those tourneys, burnished down the centuries by mystical or courtly colorings, finds its end on this last field. It submits to the saga of death, ennobles it with a clatter of arms and dust. The preeminence is no longer that of the individual; it is humanity as a whole that now leaps and succumbs, crying out its distress; it is the entirety of space which transmits the *differential* echo, the magnificent powerlessness, along with a mute entreaty, like a reminder of the thinking reed.

If the work of death, in Kojève's seminar, occupies only a limited space compared to the 'work' of History, it is nonetheless this moment of confrontation, this titanic struggle, which has impressed itself upon the collective unconscious and has resonated with successive generations. It is this celebration, aesthetic and funereal, run through with reminiscences, that Kojève's audience hears. A conjunction of magnanimity (cf. Strauss 1952: §iv, esp.: 57) and the fall, of elegance and loss, this deathly dimension is what Kojève's public recognizes above all; it was what most strongly resonated with them and has resonated down the years since. Despite what he himself has said, Kojève accentuates the romantic and febrile side of Hegel's philosophy. His hero proves himself only by an 'acceptance without reserve' (Kojève 1973: 124), by an enthrallment to 'complete and definitive annihilation' (Kojève 1973: 124) of his being. To the destruction suffered, he responds with the necessity of anguish, with a decision of finitude, inherited from Hegel. But where Hegel awaited the revelation of Knowledge and absolute philosophy, Kojève allows himself a dark and vibrant lyricism, and a surge toward Nothingness, where active forces use themselves up; a freeze-frame that evokes the magnificent combat of Consciousness and Night, in a duel of giants with gnostic resonances. Mythic and Christian influences seem to merge here, in Kojève's interpretation, into one destructive blaze, where that mysterious part of the human is glorified that turns it away from existence. Whence this magnetism, the contagious eloquence of this hymn to death? Underneath the rhetorical brilliance, no doubt the answer is to be sought in the immemorial, and the subterranean tendencies that are still molding our civilization.

BIBLIOGRAPHY

Auffret, Dominique. 1990. *Alexandre Kojève: La philosophie, l'État, la fin de l'Histoire*. Paris: Grasset et Fasquelle.

Butler, Judith. 1987. *Subjects of Desire: Hegelian Reflections in Twentieth-Century France*. New York: Columbia University Press.

Derrida, Jacques. 1982. *Margins of Philosophy*. Trans. A. Bass. Brighton: Harvester Press.

Filoni, Marco. 2010. *Le Philosophe du dimanche. La vie et la pensée d'Alexandre Kojève*. Trans. G. Larché. Paris: Gallimard.

Hegel, G.W.F. 1913. *Jenaer Realphilosophie I: Die Vorlesungen von 1803/4*. Leipzig: Hoffmeister.

———. 1979. *System of Ethical Life and First Philosophy of Spirit*. Trans. H.S. Harris and T.M. Knox. New York: SUNY Press.

Hobbes, Thomas. 1949. *De Cive or The Citizen*. Ed. P. Lamprecht. New York: Appleton-Century-Crofts.

———. 1994. *Leviathan*. Ed. E. Curley. Indianapolis and Cambridge: Hackett.

———. 2008. *The Elements of Law, Natural and Politic*. Ed. J.C.A. Gaskin. Oxford and New York: Oxford University Press.

Hollier, Denis. 1995. *Le Collège de Sociologie, 1937–1939*. Paris: Gallimard.

Jarczyk, Gwendoline, and Pierre-Jean Labarrière. 1996. *De Kojève à Hegel: Cent cinquante ans de pensée hégélienne en France*. Paris: Albin Michel.

Kant, Emmanuel. 1996. *Groundwork of the Metaphysics of Morals*. Trans. M.J. Gregor. In *Practical Philosophy*. Cambridge: Cambridge University Press.

Kojève, Alexandre. 1969. *Introduction to the Reading of Hegel: Lectures on the Phenomenology of Spirit*. Ed. R. Queneau and A. Bloom, trans. J.H. Nichols. Ithaca and London: Cornell University Press.

———. 1973. The Idea of Death in the Philosophy of Hegel: (Complete Text of the Last Two Lectures of the Academic Year 1933–34). Trans. J.J. Carpino. *Interpretation* 3/2,3, 114–156.

———. 1993. Note inédite sur Hegel et Heidegger. In *Rue Descartes* no. 7, 39.

———. 1997. *Introduction à la lecture de Hegel: Leçons sur la* Phénoménologie de l'Esprit. Ed. R. Queneau. Paris: Gallimard.

———. 1998. *L'Athéisme*. Trans. N. Ivanoff and L. Bibard. Paris: Gallimard.

Koyré, Alexandre. 1971. Hegel à Iéna. In *Études d'histoire de la pensée philosophique*. Paris: Gallimard.

Nietzsche, Friedrich. 1969. *Thus Spoke Zarathustra: A Book for Everyone and No-One*. Trans. R.J. Hollingdale. London: Penguin.

Strauss, Leo. 1952. *The Political Philosophy of Hobbes: Its Basis and Its Genesis*. Trans. E.M. Sinclair. Chicago: University of Chicago Press.

CHAPTER 3

A Pernicious Joy: *Georges Bataille*

Abstract Bataille, who attended Kojève's seminar, addresses Hegel's reasoning at its most fragile moment: when, in the dialectic of master and slave, the master himself recoils before the 'abstract death' which annihilates all consciousness. Bataille resolves the aporia by proposing a *limit-experience*, that is, a paroxysmal situation in which the subject can feel himself live and die at the same moment, on a threshold he will never cross. This hybrid formula presages the later developments of the Kojévian tragic.

Keywords Potlatch • Sacrifice • Sovereignty • Feverish chill

Of all those who attended Kojève's seminar, Georges Bataille was certainly among the most assiduous. He could not but react strongly to what Kojève offered, to its cliff-edge beauty, this manner at once precise and inspired that was Kojève's.[1] For him, however, death, which had marked his childhood and his rage to write, did not at all resemble the heroic

---

[1] On the relationship between Kojève and Bataille, the classic study is that of Michel Surya: 'It was therefore Kojève who really led him to discover Hegel, a staggering discovery, almost as staggering and moving as that of Nietzsche' (Surya 1992: 221). On the ideological differences between the two men, see Hollier (1995: 61–82).

© The Author(s) 2020
B. Rojtman, *The Fascination with Death in Contemporary French Thought*, https://doi.org/10.1007/978-3-030-47322-8_3

image offered by Kojève, this fascinating azure-blue abstraction.[2] Bataille, by his own admission, detested idealism: death for him was putrid, made of blood, savagery and gouged-out eyes.

In an article published in 1955, which he entitled 'Hegel, Death and Sacrifice,' the writer explicitly takes up Kojève's analysis and dedicates the entire first part of this study to a critical account of it. At first, one feels like going quickly through these pages, which seem to offer little that is really new for anyone who remembers the master's interpretation. In order to achieve his proper dimension, that is, his historicity as a free individual, Man must pass through death, must raise himself 'to the height of death, at whatever anguish to him' (Bataille 1997a: 282). Through death, he 'separates himself from the animal' and ceases to belong to the empire of the given 'like a stone' (1997a: 281). He enters as a priest into the ravening realm of the Negative. Death here finds again its radiant, liberating role, which shows man his truth as the exception, radically strange and off-kilter.

But let the reader make no mistake: this scrupulous fidelity of the archivist, this devotion of the acolyte who became the friend, hides a profound subversion. Though all the while seeming to follow Kojève's reasoning so closely, Bataille modulates both accent and perspective. In Kojève's version, the power of the Understanding, the force of tearing the concept away from its natural setting, aimed at a dazzling affirmation. 'The fact that some thing that is really *inseparable* from [some] other thing achieves nevertheless a separate existence' was 'miraculous' (Kojève 1973: 129, italics in the text), the miracle, indeed, of 'the existence of Man in the world' (1973: 130). And even if death were the price to pay, this sacrifice is compensated for by a singular exaltation: if access to nothingness is a destruction, at least by this storm, by this scarification, Man ensures his *ex-centricity*. At least, 'he creates for himself "an empirical existence of his own," essentially different' (1973: 130) from all others. The long effort of distanciation and dislocation had but one goal, to establish in the end 'this real world contrary-to-nature' (Kojève 1973: 130), to which only man can aspire, which only he can take upon himself, in the arid enjoyment of his

---

[2] As appendix to the cruel picture he paints of that childhood, Surya sees a Hegelian aspect to this trying period of Bataille's life: 'Georges Bataille stayed alongside his dead father, obeying, long before he knew of it, the Hegelian injunction: "Spirit is that power only to the degree in which it contemplates the Negative face to face [and] dwells with it"' (Surya 1992: 33, in italics in the text).

primacy. Only man can transcend the immediate with the flight of an eagle, even if stopped mid-course, and by 'the force, the violence of negativity,' cast himself without reserve into the 'ceaseless movement of History' (Kojève 1997: 329).

From this fervor, dedicated, in its dolor, to the great human longing, Bataille's brief account quietly distances itself. If he does occasionally underline the dynamic and masterly thrust of the seminar, it is only all the better to subtly *divert* it. To the Hegelian disincarnation, Bataille opposes a hideous death without the least epiphany. To the project of sublation, he responds with laughter and puts an end to the transformative dream. Negativity cannot be Action. The abyss is no longer a station on the way to supreme Knowledge, but a desolate, impassable boundary which condemns man to 'disappear definitively' (Bataille 1997a: 284).

To achieve his ends, under cover of orthodoxy, Bataille will thus go back to the source. For one must know how to properly read Hegel, realigning the modulations and the rhythms. The poet addresses the original text of Hegel, its muted tremors, in order to reassess its main points. Following Kojève, he revises the entire argumentation and looks specifically at the moment of crisis, at that point of aporia where the recognition by the other entails a fight to the death. In his early writings, Hegel had initially advocated a real violence, the adherence of the subject to his own annihilation: having reached its suicidal apogee, the demonstration ended with existence[3]—but not without, he thought, giving thought its ultimate test. But death, really encountered, 'in fact, reveals nothing. [...] For when the animal being supporting him dies, the human being himself ceases to be' (Bataille 1997a: 286). The death blow, rather than enlightening the consciousness, overthrows and annihilates it.

Hegel found a means to get around this impasse. In *The Phenomenology of the Spirit*, he 'abandons the paradox that he had first supported' and which made 'the *realization* of Man' depend on his 'actual death' (Kojève 1973: 152, in italics in the text). Thereafter, he holds his hero at the edge of the abyss, is satisfied to just *expose* him to the danger—without the risk ever becoming concrete. To the 'abstract negation' of a death which has really happened, he prefers the dialectic negation, within the consciousness, which '*overcomes* in such a way as to *maintain* and *conserve* the entity

---

[3] (Cf. Kojève 1973: 151), where Kojève makes explicit Hegel's position in 1803–1804: 'In contrast to "natural," purely biological death, the death that is Man is a "violent" death, at the same time self-conscious and voluntary.'

overcome' (Kojève 1997: 21, citing Hegel, in italics in the text). The abyssal peril, 'voluntarily risked' (Kojève 1973: 152), thus loses its bitter edge; it is now only a station on the Subject's path to attainment of the self. In the work of the elucidation of Spirit, it has mainly a functional, formative, role, of symbolic appropriation.

Bataille halts at this difficulty, this moment of distress where the logic of difference stumbles, and which can offer a key. For the dynamic solution proposed by Hegel seems to him to be only surface covering, hiding fermentations happening deeper within. What Bataille learns from these mortal straits is above all 'powerlessness,' that moment of shock when the entire system seems to fail, that moment of ebb, when thought, checked by the real threat of death, falls back gasping.

Bataille chooses to stop there, at this mid-way point, where one touches on forbidden games. For Bataille, immanence is the hidden lesson of dialectic. No doubt, in Hegel's view, it is possible to overcome this moment of mortal risk, to span the contradiction and continue successfully toward an end. Hegel's doctrine, in effect, 'is not only a philosophy of death'; it includes a 'tough, down-to-earth aspect,' which highlights 'class struggle and work' (Bataille 1997a: 285). But a more attentive, more alert reading should note some decisive propositions, containing the real Hegelian manifesto: no longer a metamorphosis, but a staying put, no longer History, but the here and now—of worldly life.

Sensitive to this more muted inflection, Georges Bataille holds to the paradox, without any intention to 'envisage this other side' (Bataille 1997a: 285). Against 'the monstrous energy of thought' (1997a: 283), he prioritizes the dark side of the dialectic, its mirror image in failure, what Hegel haughtily disparages as 'impotent beauty,'[4] and which Bataille will make the lynch-pin of his own struggle and his own convictions. His reading crystallizes that moment in the Hegelian logic when, faced with death, everything remains in suspense, with no conclusion and no becoming. The accent is on the '*ante*,' at the very edge, and in the terrible vision of the precipice, which transforms the meaning of the mortal process. Where the assumption of finitude should strengthen the consciousness, bring it to overcome its natural condition, this waiting signifies lethargy. In this

[4] Bataille here uses Kojève's citation (1973: 124–125) of the famous passage from Hegel's 'Preface': '[...] to uphold the work of death is the task which demands the greatest strength. Impotent beauty hates this awareness, because understanding makes this demand of beauty, a requirement which beauty cannot fulfil' (Bataille 1997a: 282).

repugnance at sublation (*Aufhebung*), there is something like a refusal to cross over, to let oneself be borne 'beyond.' Bataille keeps us at this form-less stage where the quest for supremacy cannot succeed: it comes to a halt in torpor and turns into fantasy ceremonial.

Reduced to immanence, not aiming at any end, beauty in effect is 'not susceptible to acting' (1997a: 284). It is deprived of all actual power, of any impact on life and death, only just able to preside over *entertainment* or celebration. This is why Bataille defines it, unlike in the Kojévian epic, as 'without consciousness of itself' (1997a: 285)—a desire to signify which has not succeeded, the passive echo of Understanding, its immobilization in full flight.

But as such, beauty adds luster to the bare experience of living. Its very shortcomings reverse their role, deepen: if beauty can change nothing in reality, at least it 'is,' at least it 'preserves itself' (1997a: 284) and sticks to the 'present time' (1997a: 289)—like life itself, pushed to the extreme of its a-functionality, of its contingence, a life from before determination, disjointed and aimless. Bataille gives beauty its preeminent position, of inhibition and of marvelous weakness, its exemplary position as vital prin-ciple, through its renunciation of achievement, of incitement. Because it leads nowhere, beauty, like life, like humanity, becomes its own end, 'an end' in itself (1997a: 284). Beauty, 'which seeks nothing, [...] which refuses to move itself' (1997a: 284), explores pure presence and turns away from the great epic of Spirit. She is sovereign by this forgetting, by this disinterest. She is contented, without transcending. This is why she offers a superior freedom.

This moment of letting go, so contrary to the Hegelian movement, marks the point of rupture where Bataille moves farthest from the aim of the seminar, where the acceptance of the trial, the terror of the combat, had as their only object the advent of Knowledge, that is, 'the fullness of self-consciousness' (Kojève 1973: 125). Finitude was not valuable in itself, but rather formed the ground of the activity of separation, which 'reveals the real and reveals itself' (1973: 132). If one had to be 'thinking death' and 'speaking of it' (1973: 132), it was in order to raise it to the level of Wisdom, to classify it as 'what is truly and specifically human in Man' (1973: 125)—that is, a 'discourse conscious of itself and of its origin' (1973: 132).

But this ideal death has lost its magnifying and generative force, because corrupted by the discourse that sanitizes it. Taking a position the polar opposite to that of Kojève, whose doctrine he schematizes here, Bataille denounces the rationalist concerns, the final incarnation of a logic of necessity, of constraint and of need. For, by his lights, the same sclerosis, the same stifling, rules the weight of matter and the calculations of reason. Between dialectic and beauty, the writer does not hesitate; in a sort of fever, he chooses against meaning and causality, in the name of a poetic *worklessness*.[5]

> To the extent that discourse informs it, what is *sovereign* is given in terms of *servitude*. Indeed by definition what is *sovereign* does not *serve* [*ne sert pas*]. (Bataille 1997a: 291–292, in italics in the text)

Playing on the etymology of the French verb *servir*, whereby '*ne sert pas*' means also 'is useless,' Bataille destroys the sacrificial impetuosity of the Kojévian hero. Real death can accord with nothing; thus, it coheres with nothing, is party to no advent. For 'the simple manifestation of man's link to annihilation,' the consciousness alone of a sequence or a process, would subject sovereignty 'to the primacy of servile ends' (1997a: 292). Any evidence of a logical link makes sovereignty rational and thus integrates it in the system of uses and ends. The obsession with reaching the other shore is thus also that which prevents getting to it: 'if I search for it, I am undertaking the *project* of being-sovereignly: but the project of being-sovereignly presupposes a servile being!' (Bataille 1997a: 293, in italics in the text). The reversal must be total: it maintains life, which consciousness's desire placed in danger; but it sacrifices meaning, which gave life its orientation.

If the enemy seems to have switched sides, he has not, however, changed his looks: this claim of disinterest, this indifference to salvation, which Bataille brings back into daily *life*, are they not just the last parry, a final subterfuge to counter the threat of natural determinism, to counter what its law implies in terms of rigidity, of degradation, for free will? At this point of most extreme distance, Bataille realigns indirectly with Kojève's perspective. If he attacks the logic of the negative, if he questions its central planks, it is not without subscribing, at the same time, to some anarchic presupposition of rebellion in the face of the given. Sovereignty has

---

[5] Jean-Luc Nancy understands by this term a pure exposition to the 'nothing' which is felt without being reduced: 'taking the term "incompletion" in an active sense, however, as designating not insufficiency or lack, but the activity of sharing, the dynamic, [...] of an uninterrupted passage through singular ruptures. That is to say, once again, a workless and inoperative activity' (Nancy 1991: 35).

replaced dialectic idealism, but in the name of the same impatience, the same hatred of every rule, be it mechanical or human. The argument has shifted; the rejection of Nature has changed into the rejection of the intelligible. But this is the same aesthetic of the great lord that we find in these pages, the same aristocratic mood, of disdain for fate.[6] Man is the one who does not bend, whom nothing can constrain, and whose noble silhouette looks down on the miserable struggle for life. The corollary insistence on spectacle, which is part of what is on display here, with its effusions and ramblings, reinforces the plastic and theatrical aspect of the pose: there is a proud posture that comes to us from Hobbes, an insolence of nobility, which is the distinctive mark of exceptional souls.

But this election works in the opposite direction here. Bataille defends the grandeur of man from within life, as Kojève does at the cost of man's death. It is no longer a question of combat, but of *suffering* the instant. Let go of expectation, stick to the present.[7] The strategy of withdrawal ratifies therefore an enigmatic Yes, 'stronger than all the Nos' (Nietzsche 2001: §377)—which breaks away from the future and the cadences of time. With this perseverance that has no apotheosis, it is the meaning of the human that suddenly pivots. The goal is no longer to reach, outside of oneself, against oneself, some dreadful Rubicon—but to be, to live, fixed to immediate experience: for Bataille, the 'sacrifice' 'is generally understood as the *naive form of life*, as every existence in present time, which manifests what man *is*' (1997a: 289, in italics in the text).

As against the Kojévian hero, who stayed alive because he could not do otherwise, Bataille, for his part, 'maintains his life *essentially*' (1997a: 288). What matters hereafter is no longer the instant of revelation, no longer the craggy rocks where the ego is shattered; Bataille proposes rather a 'risking' of what remains (1997a: 281), a shaking of one's entire being, which, for all that, does not tip over the cart, does not cross any boundary. Standing at the cliff edge, man is happy to just watch the misfortune, the spray of which rises up to him and wreaks its havoc on him.

---

[6] Cf. Bataille 1985: 236: 'No words are clear enough to express the happy disdain of the one who "dances with the time which kills him" for those who take refuge in the expectation of eternal beatitude.'

[7] This is what Bataille indicates, at almost the same period, in the essay 'Knowledge of Sovereignty': 'The miraculous moment [is] when anticipation dissolves into NOTHING' (1997b: 308); or 'If we live sovereignly, the representation of death is impossible, for the present is not subject to the demands of the future' (1997b: 317).

This Bataillian inversion also modifies, in its turn, the economy of the primitive 'scene.' He who, in Kojève's text, was ready to perish in overcoming his fear was the warrior or the master. But the death within, death as companion, with which one must come to terms in muted alarm, is the one glimpsed and dreaded by the slave: an extinction we draw near to one day and which leaves its sting. The master dominates it by his bravery; the slave tames it by his labor; Bataille's man alone knows it, dwells alongside it, loyal to the spirit of Hegel's 'Preface,'[8] to that which turns out to be its literal sense, its most original meaning, where is traced the necessity of a permanent disaster.

One must live, but in that ambiguous way that holds death in its nets, that shelters it and entangles it in our breath. If the writer wards off its ghastly image, it's only to make it all the more insistent and greedy. One must die, but 'while living' (1997a: 286–287), no longer with one ecstatic shudder, but—as Hegel, at bottom, no doubt wanted—over the long course of a continual dissipation. *To maintain one's life essentially,* on condition of this osmosis, of this disaggregation that soaks into the tissue, like a voracious poison. To keep his hero alive, but continually devoured, plagued by the monster that stirs under his shirt:

> If the animal which constitutes man's natural being did not die, […] if death did not dwell in him as the source of his anguish […], there would be no man or liberty, no history or individual. (1997a: 281, our italics)

In some way, Bataille here seeks to defend Hegel against himself, to demonstrate to what extent, without realizing it, 'he was right' (1997a: 289). For this underside, this more maleficent and more carnal approach, this heaviness of death before thought, is very much present in the theory—but in the background, as if filtered through a superior logic. Under the 'philosophical manner,' Bataille detects 'a personal moment of violence' (1997a: 284), a 'sensual' awareness' (1997a: 288) which shows through, to him who knows how to read it:

> Now, the life of Spirit is not that life which is frightened of death, and spares itself destruction, but that life which assumes death and lives with it. Spirit attains its truth only by finding itself in absolute disintegration. It is not that (prodigious) power by being the Positive that turns away from the Negative

[8] Cf. The citation from Hegel's 'Preface' below.

[…]; no, Spirit is that power only to the degree in which it contemplates the Negative face to face (and) dwells with it. (1997a: 282–283)⁹

In citing the famous passage in its entirety, Bataille makes it his own, revitalizes it; he relates it to a way of being, to a means of suffering the horror, of leading one's life on the borders of the unbearable. The 'dwelling' (Hegel 2018: 16) on the edge of Nothingness is an ethic, a consented-to feat of endurance. 'The life of the Spirit […] is the life that endures death and *preserves itself in it*': one must take this image at its word, prolong the confrontation like a sharper note—like living in dread, in a constancy without lull. It is no longer a question, in the view of History, of a simple 'period' to be surpassed, but rather of an existential condition, of a primordial state which one will not 'leave.' The common man, but also the romantic, the aesthete or the 'atheistic mystic' (Bataille 1997a: 294), make of this transitory phase a culmination; there they draw their breath, source their nightmares, their sleepless phantoms, in the concerted obliteration of all overcoming.

What distinguishes man from beast is therefore not just the consciousness of one's finitude, nor just the will to risk one's life. No, the man 'in truth' of Bataille is he who '*revels* in what nonetheless frightens him' (1997a: 281, our italics). The author captures this moment of 'unintelligible emotion' (1997a: 288) which spreads across the axis of time, this maintained, elementary commotion, which holds the middle ground between the realms. More than reflection, 'absolute disintegration' provokes turmoil; 'beyond discourse' it amplifies the 'shock of death' and makes it resonate (1997a: 288¹⁰), capsizing one by one the resources of coherent thought. In Bataille's view, this revelation of eternal torment, this panicked effervescence, is what best renders, *at the height of text*,¹¹ the true intention of the *Phenomenology*, its profoundly tumultuous and agonized perception: because only on this edge can life burst free, let its brutal beauty be seen, its ontological unrest.

If the exterminating Angel has departed, has given up its ennobling role, now he comes back, barbarously, into life, like a shadow growing and

---

⁹ This is another citation from the same passage from Hegel's 'Preface' which Kojève judges 'of absolutely pivotal importance' (Kojève 1973: 124–125). Cf. Hegel 2018: 16. [Translator's note: I have departed here from the translation in Bataille (1997a).]

¹⁰ [Translator's note: I have departed here from the translation in Bataille (1997a).]

¹¹ With reference to Bataille's expression, 'to the height of death' (1997a: 282).

darkening all the while. What Bataille retains from this is the *double bind*, the hybrid formula that he condenses to vanishing point, into a blaze where contraries meet: 'man must live *at the moment* that he really dies' (1997a: 287). An impossible equation, which places the accent on this overlap, on the structural contradiction of the experience of life *in the instant* that one perishes. An aporia in the accession to oneself contemporaneous with being crushed: it can only be resolved, in Bataille's privileged example, 'in the action of sacrifice' (1997a: 286).[12] For in this act of immolation, 'the sacrificer identifies himself with the animal that is struck down dead' (1997a: 287). By taking this upon himself, he gets over the walls, joins worlds together and finds himself beyond the mirror: 'And so he dies *in seeing himself die*' (1997a: 287, our italics), '*watching himself ceasing to be*' (1997a: 287, our italics).

More than by his power to die, it is by this expedient, this fiction, this turning aside of death, that man is characterized. A diversionary tactic in the face of the impracticable, a sensual substitution, where the imaginary takes over. This is the time of chimeras: what had been negating destruction has been changed into mere reflection, into a phantasm of death throes. Action turns into art, sole objective manifestation of the 'difference' sought by Hegel. 'In man it is the animal, it is the natural being, which eats. But man *takes part* in rites and performances' (1997a: 287, our italics). This new form of distinguishing man from animal is more sure, also more exciting, because invented. It is projected onto a passive register—but all the more frightful, due to its imaginary, hallucinatory effect. It is evidence of the unicity of man, but without bringing him, for all that, to a clear self-consciousness, in the sense of the glorious autonomy in which Kojève understood it. To 'willingly deceive' oneself (1997a: 287) is not the same as to 'willingly choose death.'[13] But the simulacrum by which death mimics itself, the sacrifice by which it delegates itself, the procession by which it is disguised, at least allows, by getting around the

[12] We know the troubling attraction of the idea of sacrifice for Bataille and the ambiguous place that it holds in his work. In *The Accursed Share*, Bataille described with a painstaking passion the particularly gruesome ritual practices of human sacrifice among the Aztecs (1988, Part 2:1: 'Sacrifices and Wars of the Aztecs').

[13] This expression is a slightly modified version of one used by Bataille: 'If the animal which constitutes man's natural being did not die [...] if death did not dwell in him as the source of his anguish—and all the more so in that he seeks it out, desires it and *sometimes willingly chooses it*—there would be no man or liberty, no history or individual' (1997a: 281, our italics). [Translator's note: I have departed here from the translation in Bataille (1997a).]

impasse, that one gain entry onto new soaring, baroque heights. Born of the Mystery Plays or of tragedy, 'the *sacred* horror' (1997a: 288, in italics in the text) achieves the only transfiguration possible—that is, a hypnotic and disarmed one. 'Like a theatre curtain,' it opens onto a 'beyond' (1997a: 288) made of paper—sacramental, delirious, but not *abstracted* from this world. It is doubtless no accident that the first text of Hegel's that Bataille cites bears this hallmark of the phantasmagorical. White apparitions, a 'blood-spattered head' (1997a: 279), such is the night of the world, in the eyes of the man who knows that he is mortal.

Fallen back to this side of the frontier, in a sort of endless immanence, existence maddens with the approach of the final burial. It takes on a thickness, a physical and sensual density, pregnant with all its virtualities. A sanctuary, intensely 'magical' (1997a: 283[14]), which the proximity of the negative 'enriches'[15] and throws into relief.

This is why the praise of life, of which Bataille presents such a furious image, can be conceived of only in the immediate neighborhood of death. It is the 'idea of death' that 'helps, in a certain manner and in certain cases, to multiply the pleasures of the senses' (1997a: 289). With its cadaverous shimmer, horror helps me: it revives in me the rage to exist. Associated with joy or celebration (cf. 1997a: 290), it provokes that difference in potential, this exquisitely intense excitation, which gives life its vehemence. Held back at the boundary, horror remains the very foundation of an existence doomed to annihilation, its principle of cruel exuberance. The desire for transgression surges back upon reality, makes it seethe within the limits of the possible.[16] The constraint is offset by an internal furor. It is in this excess of life, brought to incandescence, that Bataille thinks is readied the emancipatory initiation. It is through rites of devastation, bloody exorcisms, that man can finally become, in the proper sense of the term, 'the death that lives a human life' (Kojève 1973: 134).

---

[14] Bataille here uses Kojève's term (Kojève 1973: 125) citing Hegel (2018: 16).

[15] 'The man of sacrifice, on the other hand, maintains his life essentially. He maintains it not only in the sense that life is necessary for the representation of death, but [also in the sense that] he seeks to *enrich* it' (1997a: 288, italics and square brackets in the text).

[16] Bataille returns here to a mechanism already discussed in *The Accursed Share*: 'but the pressure is there. In a sense, life suffocates within limits that are too close. [...] The limit of growth being reached, life, without being in a closed container, at least enters into ebullition: without exploding, its extreme exuberance pours out in a movement always bordering on explosion' (1988: 30).

At the same time that the future closes, existence grows, becomes 'a sort of hub of the emotions' (Bataille 1997a: 289[17]). Gaiety mixes with anguish, to give 'a feverish chill' (1997a: 291) of extremes, this 'absolute disintegration' which haunted Hegel's logic, this authentic excessiveness 'where it is my joy that finally tears me apart' (1997a: 291[18]). The powers of hell awaken, everything that grows in man, of violence, of frenzy, of atrocity.

To win out over the animal, we must therefore less kill it in us than exacerbate all its forms. *Artificial jouissance*, achieved precisely at the edge of destruction. From this point of view, Bataille 'raises up' (*hebt auf*) transcendence through sin and mortal extinction through a fascination with defilement (cf. 1997a: 289). The repression of the beast no longer is achieved primarily through its immolation, but through the unbridled satisfaction, the saturation, of its instincts. Man frees himself 'of his animal needs' through contentment. And if he 'differs from the natural being' (1997a: 291), *he also is it.*

Bataille explains these ambiguous connections in another context. The distinction between life and death is made of a split that goes against nature, of a rational postulate due to human error, contrary to cosmic pulses. This distinction raises between the individual and his end a screen of anguish, which separates worlds. But a contrary movement, archaic, tempestuous, comes to sweep away these classifications. It shakes the barriers, carrying on its flood illegitimate and uncontrolled energies. It tears the singular being from his partisan unicity to give him back to the continuous.

This lava bubbles up extravagantly in an incoercible Will, brute magma, undecided, that roils its profusion. If there is a transitory, superficial and false reality that builds itself up as civilization, original *Nature* overturns it, contravenes meaning and consciousness. Nature is spendthrift, casts and wastes its being like uncounted waves, in mad generosity. Through the violence it unfurls, of eroticism or ecstasy, it is 'introducing transcendence into an organized world' (Bataille 1962: 119).

This is why it blows on us a wind of death, which calls so strongly to death. Natural life dissolves the structures and the causalities; it tears the individual away from his protective limits. Living as one dies, shredded

---

[17] [Translator's note: I have departed here from the translation in Bataille (1997a).]

[18] [Translator's note: I have departed here from the translation in Bataille (1997a), in order to maintain the wording of the Hegelian original from Hegel (2018: 16).]

from within; living in one primal, instinctual, breath, where death and sexuality merge.[19] For life itself, as Freud had already said, is only this merging, this limitless circulation, 'an orgy of annihilation' (Bataille 1962: 61). To live is to opt for death, to open oneself up to 'the huge movement made up of reproduction and death' (1962: 85–86). It is to go to one's perdition, as a stunned victim, to no longer resist, seized by some 'measureless proliferation' (1962: 113). The image of a wound in the pained flank of the hind, that flows out of us in sacred blood: we can see in all this mixture the frenzied hand of Bataille, who offers us the other aspect of decomposition, volcanic and Nietzschean—what he calls the 'gaiety' of death, not its Hegelian and tragic 'sadness' (Bataille 1997a: 290; see also Bataille 1985).

We come now to the heart of the matter. With the consciousness's withdrawal in the face of nothingness, an osmosis seems to take place, a sort of continuity of the living which establishes paths between the realms, and reduces the fracture between the organic and the human. Existence is now wedded to Nature, no longer in its deterministic aspect, which would require distance, but as profusion and as disorder. Man lives, as does the universe, in overflow and chaos. 'The naive form of life' (1997a: 289) has become another way to answer the question of the Sphinx.

If, therefore, Bataille reworks Kojève, it is to turn his idealism into pagan naturalism. If he recognizes that 'man must combat his natural impulses to violence,' this denial can only be short term: 'this signifies an acceptance of violence at the deepest level, not an abrupt break with it' (Bataille 1962: 69). His choice expresses a fidelity to the physical universe, a more anchored desire for cosmic fusion with the Earth:

> But man is not just the separate being that contends with the living world and with other men for his share of resources. The general movement of exudation (of waste) of living matter impels him, and he cannot stop it. (Bataille 1988: 23)

There is no longer, as in the Kojévian schema, a conscious and personalized tragedy, but a Dionysian harmony, where man bends to the elements, rediscovers the animal in himself. He reproduces, at his own level,

---

[19] According to Michel Surya, it is on this point that Bataille differentiates himself essentially from de Sade: 'Unlike de Sade, Bataille is not a libertine, but a *débauché*, which separates them profoundly. The eroticism which Bataille employs dirties, damages and ruins. It is tied, in advance, to an obsessional representation of death' (1992: 165; see also p. 274).

'the chemical operations of life' (1988: 27), that is, expenditure and dissolution. Like the sun, who 'gives without ever receiving' (1988: 28), he learns to spread himself generously, to disperse his rays, enduring the great wheel of infinite divisions. For if human society did at first try to ward off disorder, 'to set [itself] free from the excessive domination of death and reproductive activity,' it gives itself up now to 'the secondary influence of transgression'[20] and submits to submersion in violence.

This sovereign life, to which Bataille calls us, holds, thus, the strange luster of great devastation. It 'first pays its tribute to death' (Bataille 1962: 55)—consumed with mold, accepting corruption like its own flesh. If death submerges it from within, inhabits it without excluding it, it is because death itself has changed meaning: no longer the sign of exception, nor the fascination of otherness, but common, insignificant, as unremarkable as the numberless flies. 'Last year's have died? ... Perhaps, but *nothing* has disappeared. The flies remain, equal to themselves like the waves of the sea' (Bataille 1997a: 284, in italics in the text). Bataille's naïve man lives in the awful serenity of those who do not die, who are only exchanged one for the other: 'the dead man that the drinker [at the wake] in his turn will become shall have no other meaning than his predecessor' (1997a: 291).

In the end, we do not know whether this existence thus maintained, in the eyes of the poet, is royal or deathly. Is it the nobility of man that Bataille salutes, his capacity for liberality, his disinterest in victory? Or is it rather some instinctual dream of return to what came before, of primitive and absurd resurgence, consecrated to the dark goddess? At the frontiers of civilization, is it sin that he questions, sin as initiatory sacrilege, as an alternative to death? Bataille tells us, of violation, that it presupposes the forbidden, that is, work and ethics, but also that it surpasses in cruelty animal violence—as if this were the ultimate mark of human difference, of human transcendence. Isn't the sovereignty which he exalts subterranean, decapitated, the joyous breeding of the fly, a renunciation of death, which we don't know whether it is less implacable, less terrifying, than Kojève's renunciation of life? So, Christian god against originary paganism?[21]

[20] Cf. Bataille 1962: 83. In the face of this celebration, 'at the heart of every social bond, of violent forces, opposed to all reason,' in the face of this 'foregrounding of the "sacred," of the sacrificial,' one cannot help but ask the question, along with Bernard Sichère, of Bataille's 'vertigo' and of the 'power of attraction' which fascism, perhaps, had for him (2006: 68, 69 and 89).

[21] As if to increase the confusion, Bataille himself adds in a note: 'I imagine Catholicism closer to pagan experience' (1997a: 295 n. 10).

Archangel of separation, or syncretist divinity? We must at least pose the question of what is fermenting at the bottom of this mold, under these fantasmatic splendors, what gangrenous ideal, what inscrutable pestilence. For in Bataille's writing, whether it be liberty or damnation, 'nothing is given us that is not given in that equivocal manner' (1997a: 293).

BIBLIOGRAPHY

Bataille, Georges. 1962. *Death and Sensuality: A Study of Eroticism and the Taboo.* Trans. M. Dalwood. New York: Walker and Company.

———. 1985. The Practice of Joy in the Face of Death. In *Visions of Excess: Selected Writings, 1927–1939*, trans. A. Stoekl, 235–239. Minneapolis: University of Minnesota Press.

———. 1988. *The Accursed Share: An Essay on General Economy.* Trans. R. Hurley. New York: Zone Books.

———. 1997a. Hegel, Death and Sacrifice. Trans. J. Strauss. In *The Bataille Reader*, ed. F. Botting and S. Wilson, 279–295. London: Blackwell.

———. 1997b. Knowledge of Sovereignty. In *The Bataille Reader*, ed. F. Botting and S. Wilson, 301–312. London: Blackwell.

Hegel, G.W.F. 2018. *The Phenomenology of Spirit.* Trans. M. Inwood. Oxford: Oxford University Press.

Hollier, Denis. 1995. *Le Collège de Sociologie, 1937–1939.* Paris: Gallimard.

Kojève, Alexandre. 1973. The Idea of Death in the Philosophy of Hegel: (Complete Text of the Last Two Lectures of the Academic Year 1933–34). Trans. J.J. Carpino. *Interpretation* 3/2,3, 114–156.

———. 1997. *Introduction à la lecture de Hegel: Leçons sur la* Phénoménologie de l'Esprit. Ed. R. Queneau. Paris: Gallimard.

Nancy, Jean-Luc. 1991. *The Inoperative Community.* Ed. P. Connor and trans. P. Connor, L. Garbus, M. Holland, and S. Sawhney. Minneapolis and Oxford: University of Minnesota Press.

Nietzsche, Friedrich. 2001. *The Gay Science.* Ed. B. Williams and trans. J. Nauckhoff and A. Del Caro. Cambridge: Cambridge University Press.

Sichère, Bernard. 2006. Bataille et les fascistes. In *Pour Bataille: être, chance, souveraineté.* Paris: Gallimard.

Surya, Georges. 1992. *Georges Bataille: la mort à l'oeuvre.* Paris: Gallimard.

CHAPTER 4

An Absolute Renunciation: *Jacques Derrida*

Abstract In the wake of Bataille, Jacques Derrida takes up Kojève's reasoning but repositions it. His approach is essentially discursive and no longer existential: it raises the question of the sacrifice of meaning or of reason, not that of life itself. This deviation toward language allows Derrida to overcome the logical obstacle of real death and to push the theoretical reasoning to its limit. It makes up for this lowering of the stakes by a total renunciation and a radicalism with lyrical tones.

Keywords Laughter • Discursive • Without reserve • Sublation (*Aufhebung*) • Paul de Man

When Jacques Derrida enters the debate in his turn, and rereads Bataille, he does it in order to pit himself, through Bataille, against the giant shade of Hegel (Derrida 2001).[1] This is his singular combat, the path of sedition which he and others in the new French thought embarked on.[2] At that moment, Hegel represented the philosophic adversary *par excellence*, an

---

[1] Jacques Derrida, who was born in 1930, is a generation younger than the other authors discussed in this book. His commentary, however, directly addresses the article by Bataille which was analyzed in the preceding chapter, an article which was itself written in reference to Kojève's seminar. These three studies are thus explicitly interwoven.

[2] Derrida himself offers a rapid sketch of this evolution (cf. 'The Ends of Man,' in Derrida 1982: 115ff).

© The Author(s) 2020   43
B. Rojtman, *The Fascination with Death in Contemporary French Thought*, https://doi.org/10.1007/978-3-030-47322-8_4

image of the despotic and fascinating Father, whose 'self-evidence is a heavy burden' (Bataille 1988b: 105). Set as an epigraph to Derrida's article, this confession from Bataille's *Guilty* text sets the tone of the study: it is a question internal to the history of philosophy that Derrida is going to deal with. In order to escape the Hegelian orbit, he must pile up the paradoxes, the half-tones, the swerves and drifts, all theoretical games whose first moves he recognizes and salutes in the work of Bataille.

This approach would seem to be leading us astray from our topic. Bataille's text opened on the revelation of death: '*it is the night of the world which then presents itself to us*' (Bataille 1997: 279, our italics). But here, at least at first sight, it is no longer an issue of any clash or anguish, but of the functioning of meaning in an ideology of Reason. Death loses its nightmarish and spectral character, to become an image of erasure without appeal, an 'abstract negation'[3]; from now on it will be looked at only from this angle, in its opposition to dialectical negation—which, for its part, always saves what was put in in the first place and destroys only to 'sublate' (*aufheben*).

From this reading perspective, the lessons learned from Kojève enter a new phase: they leave their existential base to now be placed on the conceptual level. 'The drama is first of all textual,' declares Derrida (2001: 320), who goes on from there to 'reconstruct' the reflection first opened up by Bataille. There is no longer any other value, any other loss, than that of meaning. Necessarily 'significative' (2001: 321), discourse has taken over entirely. Bataille's still cautious divisions, between thought and poetry—one servile, the other sovereign, one discursive, the other ecstatic—are now pushed aside. There remains only an enemy to be faced, who contains within him all the constraints: the 'Hegelian logos' (2001: 318), its 'historical domination,' its 'enveloping resources' (2001: 317–318). Hegelianism is the monstrous hydra which smothers us in its sprawl, weighing down upon us. Derrida's appeal is therefore, in this context, all the more important because it can be a parameter for the shift in accent in this new generation: what, in the 1950s, had been seen in terms of existence or survival is here transposed into the terms of language, retranscribed and *semiotized*.

---

[3] Recall that for Hegel 'abstract negation' refers to the deadly act that effectively destroys natural life and suppresses consciousnesses. In opposition to this, the 'negation of consciousness [...] *sublates* in such a way as to *preserve* and *maintain* what is *sublated*' (cf. Hegel 2018: 79, italics in the text). In his article, Derrida speaks rather of 'abstract negativity' (2001: 322).

It is in the semantic space between Hegelian mastery and its retranslation by Bataille into sovereignty that the game is essentially won or lost. By his own admission, Derrida is interested in the 'essential displacements' which the concepts are subjected to, in their reappropriation by the writer. In order to really achieve mastery, there was classically no other route but to 'endure the anguish of death and to maintain the work of death' (2001: 321). Nonetheless, the slave wins in the end, 'who does not put his life at stake, [...] who wants to conserve his life' (2001: 321). To overcome this double requirement, death called for and refused, forbidden and necessary, Bataille proposed bridges—substitutive, imaginary forms of killing and of survival: from the book to the stage, from the sacrifice to the celebration, so many simulacra or fictions through which man can survive, though he 'thinks he is dying.' Despite these subterfuges (2001: 325–326), the author did not forget that the gesture of sacrifice implies an effective death. Ritual death, projected—but nevertheless real, where something of the primordial horror, before the bloody face of the night, imposes its violence:

> In sacrifice, the sacrificer identifies with the animal struck by death. Thus he dies while watching himself die. (2001: 325)

It is not the man, of course, who dies—it is the animal in him, by delegation; nonetheless a breath is taken from the earth, a cruelty performed, in the instant that the 'sacrificial arm' falls (2001: 325).

Jacques Derrida, like his predecessors, attacks the dialectical process at this crisis point, when the slave chooses to withdraw, when the epic of disaster is suddenly suspended. But he hollows out its vital pathos, has it turn toward more speculative concerns. The philosopher prefers to bring this critical turn in the Hegelian process back to its originary object, the coming-to-itself of consciousness. By subtle lexical shifts, he turns the sensation of physical menace toward an undermining of identity and of the system. The 'putting one's life at stake' thus becomes, in the 'history of self-consciousness,' 'a moment in the constitution of meaning' (2001: 321), which, in this totalitarian economy, will be surpassed in its turn.

If 'life has thus stayed alive' (2001: 323), this is no longer due to the reflex action of the panic-stricken body, but through a ruse *of reason*. The value to be saved, in this decisive moment, is no longer 'biological existence,' but 'an *essential* life that is welded to the first one, holding it back, making it work for the constitution of self-consciousness' (2001: 323, our italics). The organic is subordinated to 'another concept of life'—aseptic, neutralized and more in conformity with the needs of a no-residue theoretical reflection. Thus, the philosopher prefers to hold to the intellectualist, properly logical, aspect of the demonstration: if man, for Hegel, possesses a grandeur, it comes from his thought; death appears fearsome in so far as it compromises the hegemony of consciousness. The dialectic of risk, adroitly reconstructed in Derrida's reading, keeps as close as possible to the metaphysical; it is not his own end that the subject senses in a flash, but, more ideally, the end of his *truth*:

> Hegel clearly had proclaimed the necessity of the master's retaining the life that he exposes to risk. Without this economy of life, the 'trial by death, however, cancels both the truth which was to result from it, and therewith the *certainty of self* altogether.' To rush headlong into death pure and simple is thus to risk *the absolute loss of meaning*. (2001: 322, our italics)

With his well-known ingeniousness, Derrida cancels out the visceral terror of nothingness, incriminating, rather, the perseverance of the subject, who aims for 'the conservation, the circulation and the reproduction *of self as of meaning*' (2001: 323, our italics).[4] At no point does his exegesis reconsider this first term: *self*-reproduction. As if it were understood that existence, in its trembling, escaped reflection from the outset, that it could not, as such, be sacrificed. Surreptitiously, the urgency of natural life thus moves into the background.[5] It is a given: one does not enter into discussion on the irrefutable. What focuses attention, what continues to scandalize, are the parasitic claims of the spirit, dissimulated behind biology: no longer to live, but to live *for*, no longer to feel or breathe—but to know:

> What is laughable is the *submission to the self-evidence of meaning*, to the force of this imperative: that *there must be meaning*, that nothing must be definitely lost in death, or further, that death should *receive the signification* of 'abstract negativity.' (2001: 324, our italics, except 'submission')

---

[4] [Translator's note: I have departed here from the translation in Derrida (2001).]

[5] In fact, the movement from mastery to sovereignty restores the importance of natural life: 'for the sovereign operation *also needs life* [...] in order to be in relation to itself in the pleasurable consumption of itself' (2001: 324, our italics). But Derrida quickly resolves this difficulty, never to return to it again.

If Derrida agrees with Bataille in his analysis, it is in order to overdetermine it, all the better to denounce, via this adjustment, the brusque evasion of Hegel, his miserable recourse to sublation (*Aufhebung*), which, though it 'conserves the stakes' (2001: 323), eludes the difficulty. Derrida's commentary, under these conditions, can easily outline the dodge that has taken place: in this stylized form, the Hegelian spiral of negation can be attacked head-on, directly taken to task. The desire for 'reproduction of meaning' symbolizes on its own the inconsistency, the absolutism, of the rationalist utopia.

Under cover of this skewed allegiance, Derrida takes advantage of the fact that Bataille situates his reflection *on this side* of death, in the ambiguity of a confrontation that never actually takes place. He adroitly exploits this region—which Bataille had placed under the auspices of sacrifice, of gaiety and of anguish. If he prefers to effectively hide the barbarism of the contact with the knife, he nevertheless retains, from the simulacrum and the trial which is play-acted in it, some undeniable advances: the mismatch of the limit-experience and any 'phenomenology of spirit,' its power to throw that phenomenology off-kilter. The 'burst of laughter from Bataille' (Derrida 2001: 323) underlines the happiness of an alert perspicacity, at the moment when 'everything covered by the name lordship collapses into comedy' (2001: 323). Inherited from Nietzsche, laughter is there, primarily, to decry the sleight of hand of the 'sublation' and the false power of reason. It alone 'exceeds dialectics and the dialectician' (2001: 323). It alone withdraws the sovereign operation 'from the horizon of meaning and knowledge' (2001: 323), and is key to a rebellion still alive, that widens the difference between mastery and sovereignty.

Isn't Bataille in fact the man of dissidence and revolutions, who rejects, no less than his successors, the hold of the system, who also wants to 'escape' any discursive 'prison,' and dedicates himself to the sole project of 'escap[ing] the project' itself (Bataille 1973: 60)?

Against the intention, against the aim of an end, which stifles real thought and '*suspends* anguish,' 'inner experience' must remain a 'denunciation of the truce' (Bataille 1988a: 46, italics in the text).[6] Against the supreme hope, laughter remains the last resort: it tears apart the logical illusion, it lays bares our weakness and whispers its conviction, that 'our will to arrest being is damned' (Bataille 1988a: 91).

---

[6] [Translator's note: Bataille (1988a: 59) does not translate this line.]

It is this constant rejection, like an allergic reaction, of any constraint, that Derrida echoes here. Citing his predecessor at length, he joins him in castigating 'the verbal servitude of reasonable being' (Bataille 1988a: 115), the *currish docility* of the 'I,' who humbly pretends to universality (1988a: 115). Between the two men, there is the complicity of a shared protestation, a shared impatience, a shared concern to have done with 'discursive intelligence' (1988a: 115).

But this bias toward meaning obviously decenters the message; it clearly distorts Bataille's stormy, excessive work. For there is, for the poet, a rage in writing which brings even language itself to the point of explosion, a disorder in the extreme, which gnaws at life in its quivering heart. If Bataille intends, as Derrida notes, to proscribe 'reason, intelligibility,' the sack which he glorifies does not stop at these ramparts; it rumbles on and spreads, carrying with it 'the ground itself' (Bataille 1988a: 134) and the universe.

On the sacrificial pyre, it is all of existence that burns, regardless of its modes. If one must reach sovereignty, it is in 'the depth of terror,' at the level of the unknown, at 'the extreme limit where he [man] succumbs' (Bataille 1988a: 134). 'The trial of "torture"' (Bataille 2001: 78) thus escapes all intellection or formalization. It can only germinate from a brute and *continuous* substrate (cf. Bataille 2001: 78),[7] foreign to any linguistic sequence, in a 'sovereign silence that *articulated language interrupts*' (Bataille 2001: 90, in italics in the text[8]). Speech itself seems to collapse, washed away by the flood. 'Joy of the dying man, wave among waves. Inert joy of the dying, of the desert, fall into the impossible' (Bataille 1988a: 51). In these confines impossible to formulate, where God himself dies as man, 'words, their sickest games, *cannot suffice*' (1988a: 135, our italics). For Bataille, 'anguish *is no less than* intelligence the means for knowing, and the extreme limit of the "possible," [...] *is no less life* than knowledge' (1988a: 39, our italics).

Before so much blind exaltation, such assertions of ignorance, one must ask, following Derrida's critique, what could have pushed such a sensitive reader to thus flatten out the asperities in Bataille's text. Panicked, pre-conceptual fear of annihilation, the raw torment of survival, seem here relegated to the margins of the controversy. Everything Bataille had revivified of the dialectic, its chasms, its impasses, finds itself shrunken down to

---

[7] On this theme, see also Bataille (1988a: 93–96).

[8] [Translator's note: I have departed here from the translation in Bataille (2001).]

the rational outline. One must ask, why such 'avarice,' such concern to hold to the *discreet*, to this Hegelian bed of Procrustes where Derrida lays down the phantasms, the ecstasy, the overabundance, which Bataille had made the breeding ground of his own unreason.

Perhaps one can only answer if one discerns, under this cramping up of reasoning, the profound metamorphosis which this flatness induces, if one imagines that, through this parsimony, an experience of the extreme might be shared. As if, through the straits of the concept alone, by its dialectical ruggedness, Derrida were to rejoin Bataille, whose violence has seduced him.

For in changing register, the ordeal of sacrifice has been modified: related to discourse, it gains 'seriousness'; it finds itself at last lived to the end, authentically celebrated. The devitalization of point of view allows one to break through the blockage—of 'abstract death'—at once the end of the process of the revelation of consciousness to itself and the end of natural being. By focusing only on the intelligible and meaningful aspect of the final hour, Derrida breaks the log jam; he uses the obstacle itself in order to go beyond it, to cross a threshold which the biological had to respect. Absolute negation, logically untenable, can now be thought. For one can live in *absolute* renunciation of meaning (Derrida 2001: 323); one can live *and* die at once if one only has to die in spirit. On this terrain, Derrida finds a tone and a Romantic radicalism which seem to come straight from the lectures of the young Hegel at Jena. When corporeality has become subsidiary, veering toward essence, there is no time for hesitation. One has to set out, break a lance against the enemy. Where Hegel, then Kojève, and even Bataille, had stepped back, in a more or less delightful fear, the Young Guard of the 1960s intends to keep on to the very end. It is no longer the life of man, but the image of man, as it has been understood from the dawn of metaphysics, as humanism has nurtured it, that is now to be crushed.[9] Man's vertigo is here redefined, the unhappiness of the consciousness—all that which, we thought, brings us into accord with

---

[9] In his study on 'The Ends of Man,' Derrida calls for a necessary 'sublation' of humanism, which he makes into one of the major lines of opposition between his intellectual generation and the preceding one: 'The anthropological reading of Hegel, Husserl and Heidegger was a mistake in one entire respect, perhaps the most serious mistake. [...] The *Phenomenology of Spirit* [...] does not have to do with something one might simply call man' (Derrida 1982: 117). And, further on: 'Just as, according to Husserl, one may imagine a consciousness without soul (*seelenloses*), similarly—and a fortiori—one may imagine a consciousness without man' (1982: 118).

ourselves and makes us human, is now jeopardized: we must follow the progress of this movement to the limit, of this joyous transgression that gets carried away and crosses over, now free, rid of the ballast of the miserable precautions of understanding, which see the paladin's courage fail him.

It quickly appears in effect that the shift in perspective moves the debate to its most demanding level. Contrary to dialectical negation, which 'enslaves itself' (Derrida 2001: 323) only all the better to dominate, the revelatory laughter allows a negativity without restraint and without compensation, which gives the confrontation back its grandeur. No longer restrained by any vital interest, no economic calculation, sovereignty represents this altered form of mastery which surpasses the logic of conservation. Tied to signification, sovereignty can afford to go toward a 'death pure and simple'; it can risk 'mute and nonproductive' death (2001: 322). It exposes itself exemplarily to 'absolute loss' (2001: 322), in so far as this defeat, strictly speaking, is that of meaning.

Protected by this reframing, the demonstration becomes ever more incisive, the stances become singularly polemic and passionate: '*It does not suffice* to risk death [...] Sovereignty must still sacrifice lordship and, thus, the *presentation* of the meaning of death. For meaning, when lost to discourse, is *absolutely destroyed and consumed*' (2001: 330, our italics, except 'presentation'). If Hegel's mistake was to want to '[give] meaning to death' (2001: 324), this ambition itself slows his momentum, discourages him from giving himself entirely to 'the experience of the sacred, to the *reckless sacrifice* of presence and meaning' (2001: 325, our italics[10]). Denouncing this prudence, Derrida insists rather on the imperative of complete abandon, of a total devotion to loss. To block 'the submission to the self-evidence of meaning' (2001: 324), he becomes advocate for Bataille, whose 'comicalness' is part of a real anguish, of an 'expenditure *with no hope of return* [...] *without reserve*' (2001: 324, our italics[11]). It is this shift to the extreme that transmutes mastery into sovereignty, 'when it ceases to fear failure and is lost as the *absolute* victim of its own sacrifice' (2001: 335). As if it required the asceticism of unhappiness to reach the supreme sacrament, by suddenly *letting go*. Reactualized as simulacrum,

[10] [Translator's note: I have departed here from the translation in Derrida (2001).]

[11] [Translator's note: I have departed from the translation of this last phrase in Derrida (2001).]

the dispossession now regains something of its mythic violence, of a cathartic and barbaric immolation.

One cannot but be astonished at such an escalation, under the pretext of a hermeneutic approach, as if fascinated by the absolute. The sacrifice of concepts must be 'pitiless' (2001: 338), the loss 'useless, senseless' (2001: 342, citing Bataille 2001: 284 note). The trace is a trace 'only if presence is irremediably eluded in it [...] if it constitutes itself as the possibility of absolute erasure' (2001: 336). In a sort of mutilating giddiness, this radicalism admirably transposes, in the mode of deconstruction, the tones of vehemence ushered in by Bataille:

> To go 'to the end' both of 'absolute rending' and of the negative without 'measure,' without reserve, is not progressively to pursue *logic* [...] On the contrary, it is convulsively to tear apart the negative side. (2001: 328, in italics in the text)

One can glimpse, under the concept, the metaphoric effect of laceration, a frenzy of the image which veers toward poetry. As if the transfer over to the sign allowed the liberation of underlying affects, a blaze *à la Bataille*, which the confrontation with the real had repressed. For Derrida, as for Bataille, 'the destruction of discourse' becomes a crazy escapade, 'a kind of potlatch of signs that burns, consumes, and wastes words in the gay affirmation of death' (Derrida 2001: 347). The biological impunity granted by the shift to speculation leaves the field open to a paroxysmal expression, which unfolds with all its force for enchantment.

Reading these fiery lines, where the sacrifice of spirit is celebrated—with no victim or any splash of blood—one cannot but yield, however, to a certain perplexity. Is the suspending—or perhaps dodging—of mortal peril the price to be paid for this intransigence, for this fall without a net, meteoric and yet benign, in these years when the memory of the war is receding, when French thought is becoming abstract and reflexive? Existence has faded into an ancillary, incidental phenomenon. Reduced to having to 'simulate [...] the absolute risk' (2001: 324), it enters only as a secondary factor within the obscure movement of the sovereign operation. Is this to say that 'real' death, this nothingness 'that gnaws [...] from within' (Bataille 1997: 280), this hallucinatory folly which Bataille glimpses behind Hegelian reason, has been swept away? One does not know whether this inflection toward meaning, into which the whole problematic topples, denatures or, rather, uncovers the deep motifs of the provocation unto death. Are we witnessing a veritable transformation of philosophical interests? Or should we rather recognize in this reinterpretation a disguised variant of the original existential demand, its written form, that is, its secondary and powerless formulation? So does this conceptual displacement express rupture or continuity? Projected onto discourse, cut off from its anthropological roots, has the entire Hegelian approach been sharpened—or blunted? The question becomes critical when we consider that it is precisely at this point of suture, between life and life, between body and meaning, that the transition takes place from one philosophical generation to the next, from existentialism to deconstruction.

At least the drift toward commentary, in removing the direct threat, in stiffening the Hegelian framework, allows hidden effects to be brought to light, which the weight of terror kept hidden. It unleashes related values, already inscribed in the primordial scene, but which were subdued by the brute need to live. If sovereignty wins out in the end, if it really is this sought-after form of 'expenditure' that nothing stops anymore, it is doubtless because, when transferred under the species of meaning, it meets parallel aspirations, which were at the outset less directly perceptible, but which, suddenly brought to light by the textual mode, become little by little noticeable under the logical argument: the expectation of liberty, of a heady anarchy, which hangs onto death like onto the hems of some marvelous garment.

A driver of emancipation, sovereignty's 'primary characteristic' (Derrida 2001: 334) is that it escapes all grasp as it does all designation: it *'does not govern itself.* And does not govern in general: it governs neither others, nor things, nor discourses' (2001: 334, in italics in the text). Contrary to mastery, which is always subordinate to its own victory, always concerned about the meaning it wants to maintain, sovereignty is uncontrollable: it 'owes nothing' (2001: 335[12]), 'is attached to nothing,' does not try to 'maintain itself' (2001: 334). It is a sensitive divinity, magnificently evasive, which always 'eludes [...] expectation' (2001: 340) and breaks the ties of any desire. This stormy insistence on never being taken or 'conditioned' (2001: 340) points to a symbolic nub. It gives the sovereign operation a rare aura of refusal to submit and a disquieting prominence. It has an emancipating role, going as far as an obsession, a concern for individuality, a vow of ingratitude (2001: 340) which rejects all law. This is no longer Kojévian liberty, which posited the grandeur of man, but an

---

[12] [Translator's note: I have departed here from the translation in Derrida (2001).]

irrepressible, as if physiological, need for evasion, fluidity, wild autonomy. Part of this posture is, no doubt, a question of temperament—but also a phenomenon of the age. The Law has become obsolete, authority unbearable. The revolt against natural determinism has changed into a rejection of all constraints, and first of all that of meaning, of imposable and delineated meaning, like an old-fashioned dogma.

This sudden incandescence, at that point where Derrida denounces the master's pusillanimity, shows the importance of the question. What's more, the libertarian vow seems to demand some violence in order to establish itself. It is only in excess that the last ties are broken, that the ship can set sail. Only the terror of sacrifice guarantees an unequivocal independence. The loss must go to the very core in order to really be a loss, absolutely desolate and floating, absolutely 'without relation'[13]: 'It is unfortunate to possess no more than ruins,' Bataille had already said, 'but this is not any longer to possess *nothing*; it is to keep in one hand what the other gives' (Derrida 2001: 331, citing Bataille 1988a: 148, our italics). Only a disordered 'non-meaning,' thwarting all markers, can bring us 'beyond [...] closure' (2001: 339), can give sovereignty back its efficacy. All compromise in one's demands, all recognition of grounded values, would lead to the trap of a new conditioning. Renounce oneself, renounce being recognized, 'lose consciousness' (2001: 335) right to the heart of all knowledge, of all interior memory. Negation pushed to its end thus becomes an end in itself, its only allegiance that to itself. 'Absolutely adventurous,' sovereign writing can 'assure us of nothing' (2001: 346); it has no goal—but also, by the same token, is absolutely unruly, trembling, absolutely irresponsible and wayward.

As the demonstration progresses, almost despite itself, it takes on an astonishing lyricism. The image wins out over the argument. A vagabond vision of the bird-man, free of all weight. The ontological torment seems to have been exchanged for a more ethereal, immaterial dream, for a debt-free floating which tells only of the pride of the dispossessed man. The feverish indictment reveals an ancient mirage, of a troubled and deleterious beauty. In its turn, the Derridian word seems drawn to myth, its metaphysical fervor, its age-old absolutism—as if it drew thence its exorbitance and its justification.

---

[13] 'To relate the major form of writing to the sovereign operation is to institute a relation in the form of a non-relation' (2001: 339).

This strange magnetism, however, does not really blind the philosopher, whom a perpetual state of alert keeps on the watch against the temptation of the negative *in itself*: a non-dialectical negative, close to laughter and libertarian—but which still enchants, in its finery of nothingness. This new danger, no less alienating than the other, is that of stunned stupefaction: the subversive push tends to ossify, to be reified as excess, caught in the ice of a lofty adoration. Pushed to the level of stupor, the sacrificial drive, with all that sustains it, all that burns and liberates, has generated its own trap: the recklessness of loss throws the supplicant into the nets of that which so resembles a new theology that one could mistake it for one—even if only a negative one, even if a theology haunted by difference.[14]

While extolling the ousting of meaning, Derrida continues to be wary of an anarchic abuse that would see sovereignty handed up to 'a game without any rules' (Derrida 2001: 330, citing Bataille 2001: 95[15]). Its poetry thus risks being caught, frozen in its excess, allowing itself by the same token to be 'domesticated, "subordinated," better than ever' (2001: 330). Very early on in his reflection, the leader of the troops understood that the path of revolt was cut off, that at the end of the dialectic, 'philosophy, in completing itself, could both include within itself and anticipate all the figures of its beyond, all the forms and resources of its exterior' (2001: 318). As if there were no ultimate undermining because of this endless succession of binary 'recuperations,' as if there were no means, even by violence, of escaping the Hegelian embrace.

Unless one thinks negation beyond all structure, in an obliqueness which 'exceeds the oppositions' (2001: 319), and shifts the concepts 'outside the symmetrical alternatives in which, however, they seem to be caught' (2001: 344[16]). To be and not to be, to exclude and to remain. 'The non-meaning of the sovereign operation is neither the negative of, nor the condition for, meaning, *even if it is this also*' (p. 344, our italics, except 'also'). So each proposition allows a corrective, splits, lives together with its contrary. A *non-negative* deletion which paralyzes all truth and thwarts dialectic by disorienting it.

---

[14] Derrida adds that, if, 'in order to shake the security of discursive knowledge,' Bataille's *general writing* 'indicates itself as mystical' (2001: 344), the reader would be wrong to hold to this rough evaluation, which misses the text's more winding and errant pathways. [Translator's note: I have departed here from the translation in Derrida (2001).]

[15] [Translator's note: I have departed here from the translation in Derrida (2001).]

[16] [Translator's note: I have departed here from the translation in Derrida (2001).]

The end of the article is thus strewn with restrictions and antinomies,[17] where a properly Derridian '*double bind*' comes to light. A-logicism emerges as the desired form of 'expenditure' which escapes binarity, a 'contradictory overprint,' whose difficult necessity the philosopher announced in the opening lines of his essay. For, in its ambiguity, sovereign writing 'is neither true nor false, neither truthful nor insincere. It is purely *fictive* in a sense of this word that the classical oppositions of true and false, essence and appearance, lack' (2001: 439–440, n. 34, italics in the text).

It is the tactic of deconstruction that comes back into play here: by discrete ruses and successive manipulations, it '[folds] discourse into strange shapes' (2001: 319), makes it 'slide' (2001: 333) in the tangle of yes and no, of speech and silence. It makes every word tremble, shakes concepts out of their initial understanding, causing them to be affected and to deviate, drowning 'immeasurably' (2001: 338). And the tactic of deconstruction mobilizes, to this end, techniques of evasion when closest to the enemy's *massed body*, techniques from within, when closest to the shackles of logic and meaning. No longer to combat, burn, destroy, but to flow, winding one's way, covering one's tracks, to again, relentlessly, 'make sense slide, to denounce it or to deviate from it' (2001: 344–345). The system cannot be shaken by rupture, but only by drift: crumbling toward chance, accident or play—without writing producing any new 'predicates' (2001: 337), without anything being erased, engulfed by the negative or absence; there remains only this pure movement back and forth, this silken undoing which surprises and absolves:

> The instant […] slides and eludes us between two presences. […] It […] carries itself off in a movement which is simultaneously one of violent effraction and of vanishing flight. (2001: 333)

Erotic power of this slightest of seditious touches, lovingly parasitic, which inflects 'the old body' of language (2001: 334).[18] Like a Borgesian labyrinth condensed into a straight line, the flight is invisible—denials,

---

[17] 'The writing of sovereignty […] withdraws itself from every theoretical or ethical question. *Simultaneously, it offers itself to these questions* on its minor side' (pp. 439–440, note 34, our italics). 'The concepts of general writing *can be read only on the condition* that they be deported, shifted outside the symmetrical alternatives *from which, however*, they seem to be taken, and in which, *after a fashion, they must also* remain' (p. 344, our italics).

[18] [Translator's note: I have departed from the translation in Derrida (2001).]

affirmations and refutations, a series of displacements that create an illusion, and ensure only the lucidity of the separation. Without breaking anything from the outside, without submitting anything: to disappoint above all, in a perpetual escape that ebbs or overflows. So that in the end there will be no more 'sovereignty *itself*' (2001: 342, our italics). 'Like general economy,' the writing of sovereignty *is* not[19]; it can only *be* loss, or more exactly, '*relation* to loss of meaning' (2001: 342, our italics).

It is therefore under the sign of this *indifference*[20] that the sovereign operation, revisited by Derrida, eludes petrification, its condensation into an idol; it is an indecision in the second degree, which, not content to 'neutralize [...] all contradictions,' even manages to transgress this neutrality, this whiteness that is too colored, too imbued with 'negative essence' (2001: 346). 'Neither positive nor negative' (2001: 327), sovereignty in its full effect is atonal, 'has no identity' (2001: 335). It renounces even erasure and the privilege of 'its own risk' (2001: 334). Nothing can any longer surprise it, comprehend it or enclose it. It is elsewhere, beyond, ends nowhere, is unlike any recognizable, identifiable land. One glimpses something indefinable, an unexplored country, *vague effusions* (cf. Bataille 2001: 94)—above what can be conceived, what man can yet formulate. It is absence met, the impossible touched, a 'speech which maintains silence' (Derrida 2001: 332): that is, this archaic, unfindable reverse side, this *continuum* (Derrida 2001: 333) where everything 'streams' within and without (Bataille 1988a: 94), in a homogeneity that is pre-categorial and without plenitude.[21]

Thanks to its meanders, this Derridian meditation in the second degree, which denigrated even death, seems thus to lead us to an exaggerated, impracticable form of liberation. Like a hunger for space, febrile, born of initiatory tales, a desire for liberty fed on myths of Icarus. Don't the ocean winds, greater than us, resound like the distant echo of an incoercible aspiration to transgress the limits of being, to walk in the steps of the pale

---

[19] It is Bataille—as Derrida indicates—who underlines the word.

[20] Cf. Bataille (2001: 91): 'The sovereign operation is arbitrary and although its effects legitimate it [...], it is indifferent to judgement in this respect,' or also (2001: 216) 'not only does the sovereign operation not subordinate itself to anything, it is indifferent to the effects that may result.' [Translator's note: I have departed here from the translation in Bataille (2001).]

[21] Derrida continues here the theme of 'communication' initiated by Bataille in *Inner Experience* (1988a: 93–98).

stranger, of this adolescent vision 'with no ties,' 'floating onward into the promising immensity of it all' (Mann 2005: 142)?

And yet, from this far-off 'splashing foam' (Bataille 1988a: 95), like the assassin to the scene of the crime, Derrida seems to want to return—to come back again to the 'fragile walls' (Bataille 1988a: 95) of discourse: law, truth, 'the closure of knowledge' (Derrida 2001: 442 n. 48). From close to the breath or spirit of Bataille, whose rhythm it takes up, Derrida's writing retracts again, shrinks to the field of History and work; while it 'deconstitutes' them, it admits their necessity as prior and constituent (cf. Derrida 2001: 341). As if, in order to ensure 'the erasure without return, of all meaning' (2001: 341[22]), one had to keep drawing energy, invariably, hypnotically, from the Hegelian 'sublation,' recognize it in order to counter it.

Doubtless, it is a matter, for Derrida, of interpreting Bataille against Bataille, of using dialectic from back to front one last time, in order the better to corrupt it. Far from enclosing the sublation itself in the limits of the system, it transforms it in 'heightening' it: removes it from the register of 'work' and empties it of all determination (cf. Derrida 2001: 348). Thus rendered blind and oblique, the negating structure describes the pure passage, a 'transgressive relationship' (2001: 349) as such, which marks for Derrida the surpassing of the 'world of meaning' toward non-meaning. It is then the logic of speculation as a whole which is perverted, by the very means which were meant to underlie it:

> [...] an intraphilosophical concept, the speculative concept par excellence, is forced to designate a movement which properly constitutes the excess of every possible philosopheme. (2001: 349)

But beyond the technical virtuosity, in this paradoxical reversal, some final veil is lifted. It's now philosophy as such which enters the orbit of the 'natural or naïve consciousness' (2001: 349): the pretention to meaning has become a way of still living according to instinct, of getting bogged down in the brute givens of human hope. To go beyond will therefore be to overcome, in Kojève's way, the still 'natural and vulgar' desire for the 'circulation of meaning and value' (2001: 349). An irrepressible desire like that of survival, and which only death constrains. The rattle of lost combats. A desire for meaning, like the reproachful eye in the tomb, watching

---

[22] [Translator's note: I have departed here from the translation in Derrida (2001).]

Cain (in Hugo's poem), and that only the horror of the grave transfigures. The approach of Night allows us to finally 'see,' to 'emerge' (2001: 349, citing a passage from Bataille 2001: 85) out of the vital and its logical constraints, thrown as we are upon the alternative of submission or Nothingness:

> Thus, there is the vulgar tissue of absolute knowledge and the mortal opening of an eye. A text and a vision. The servility of meaning and the awakening to death. (2001: 350)

Unhappiness has reclaimed its place, the heroic ride, toward absolute destruction. Against the 'servility of meaning,' a more august mastery arises, more purely hopeless. Brought back to the starting point's aporia, and setting out again on the route of legend, Derrida shows here to what extent he belongs to the long tradition of the quest. But, from deep within this affiliation, still differentiating himself from it, he gives death a more arid majesty, that was slumbering within its ancient forms. Twenty years after *Writing and Difference*, having cast off his semiotic robes, he will describe in clear terms, at once searing and inspired, the flashing shock of the ultimate encounter, the epiphany of the irremediable, 'the light of this incinerating blaze where nothingness appears.' Faithful to 'disbelief,' he will write of the awakening to death and its 'blaze,' the 'terrifying lucidity' of the end (Derrida 1989: 21). These pages of mourning, tremblingly impassioned for a friend 'gone forever' (1989: 21), radiating in their turn, superbly, 'the dark light of the sun' (1989: 25).

For this death in us, this memory in us of death, 'greater and older than us' (1989: 37), pushes our frail barks toward the incommensurable. It is the Other within us, greater than us, greater than 'what […] we can bear, carry, or comprehend' (1989: 33). A death beyond, 'inadequate to itself' (1989: 37), a-symbolic and measureless. 'Beyond any quantitative comparisons,' it is the non-totalizable trace, which crosses over, becomes limitless, 'defying all reappropriation' (1989: 38). In this excess, the philosopher connects to some private devastation which swells within us, which works upon us and makes us infinite from within, offered up to be devoured by the immensity. And if death is the price of this unnumberable, already within us, that tears and streams—let death be, and grief, let them hollow out their way, in to the heart of us. If Derrida refuses the heroic and controlled end, it is no doubt that this immaculate experience, already complete, closed off, is not the ungraspable, the rarefied unbearable event that his ontology aspires to. Close to negative theology—which Derrida rejects however (cf. Derrida 2001: 343–344), because still insufficiently fluid, insufficiently porous to the starry gulf—close to the Kabbalah, which sweeps the consciousness up into celestial routes, Derridian iconoclasm is of an unequaled purity, raised to a level of demands where nothing is like anything known, where nothing can be recognized. An iconoclasm dedicated to an infinite that knows no bounds, that surrounds us and constitutes us. Derrida, despite himself, affected, dazzled, comes under the influence of this Uncanny, within-without, knowing nothing but nothingness. Like Abraham, indiscriminately destroying the idols in the mythical museum of the human, leaving nothing in its wake but an unpronounceable No.

BIBLIOGRAPHY

Bataille, Georges. 1973. *L'expérience intérieure*. Paris: Gallimard.

———. 1988a. *Inner Experience*. Trans. L.A. Boldt. New York: SUNY Press.

———. 1988b. *Guilty*. Trans. B. Boone. Venice Beach, CA: Lapis.

———. 1997. Hegel, Death and Sacrifice. Trans. J. Strauss. In *The Bataille Reader*, ed. F. Botting and S. Wilson, 279–295. London: Blackwell.

———. 2001. Method of Meditation. In *The Unfinished System of Nonknowledge*, 77–99. Minneapolis: University of Minnesota Press.

Derrida, Jacques. 1982. *Margins of Philosophy*. Trans. A. Bass. Brighton: Harvester Press.

———. 1989. *Memoirs for Paul de Man, Revised Edition*. Trans. C. Lindsay, J. Culler, E. Cadava, and P. Kamuf. New York: Columbia University Press.

———. 2001. From Restricted to General Economy: A Hegelianism without Reserve. In *Writing and Difference*, trans. Alan Bass, 317–350. London: Routledge.

Hegel, G.W.F. 2018. *The Phenomenology of Spirit*. Trans. M. Inwood. Oxford: Oxford University Press.

Mann, Thomas. 2005. *Death in Venice*. Trans. M.H. Heim. London: HarperCollins.

CHAPTER 5

The Desire for Indifference: *Maurice Blanchot*

Abstract Under the aegis of Bataille, Blanchot in his turn criticizes the dialectic process, whose final and totalizing stage he calls into question. The *passion of negative thought* brings man to reiterate his questioning indefinitely, against all plenitude. Beyond the absolute, it pushes him toward an 'outside the whole' which is neither death nor life and where nothing is ever resolved. The limit-experience thus becomes a paradoxical experience, which is representative of the Blanchotian universe: negation without negation; death impossible to die; dispossessed belonging.

Keywords Limit-experience • Levinas • Decisive contestation • Worklessness • Eurydice

In a brief and serious reflection on the passion of the negative, Maurice Blanchot pays homage to the man who, alongside Emmanuel Levinas, was his closest friend. Acknowledging in Georges Bataille the 'singularity' of an 'extraordinary mind' (Blanchot 1993: 203), he opts to approach Bataille's work, the glow of his writing and its subversiveness, from the angle of the Hegelian dialectic. The task of the critic's 'accompanying discourse' (1993: 203), according to Blanchot, is to find the reading perspective which is most effective, that is, which is most faithful, most 'innocent' (1993: 203), preserving thought. On the fringes of the canonical texts, in *Inner Experience* or *Guilty*, it is therefore the Hegelian

© The Author(s) 2020   61
B. Rojtman, *The Fascination with Death in Contemporary French Thought*, https://doi.org/10.1007/978-3-030-47322-8_5

inheritance, its negating and stimulating force, that he prefers to address first, in order to reveal the foundations of the Bataillian exceptionalism. This choice is indicative of a certain familiarity: though there is no doubt that Blanchot was not among the regulars at 'the seminar,' he felt its seduction nonetheless. His closeness to Levinas, and especially to Bataille, draws him irresistibly, though indirectly, to the Kojévian problematic, of which he will be one of the most astute analysts.

Thus, it is that his reading, always subtle and painstaking, follows Bataille's account of Kojève's analysis (cf. Bataille 1997a). As he traces its windings, Blanchot underlines the ambiguity of an apparent veneration that goes from awed acknowledgment to quiet sedition. But this perceptible reversal, as he endeavors to show, is fundamentally only the result of a conceptual purism: in pushing the Hegelian demonstration to its conclusion, the disciple does no more than reveal its paradox. If Hegel, as Bataille puts it, really 'did not know to what extent he was right' (1997a: 289), this is because a profound inspiration within him won out, by its high mindedness, over the declared aim; one only had to reinstate the rigor, to take seriously this subterranean exigency, in order to unearth its true greatness. One has only to follow its logic beyond the stage where Hegel, deceived by his own genius, had had to stop. If 'contestation' remains the first principle and the motor that 'traverses all of history' (Blanchot 1993: 204), it has the weakness that, in its consecrated form, in the end it dissolves itself. Rather than drawing our attention to the process, or to the moment of abeyance, it presents the absolute in a sun-struck stupor that crushes man in its majesty.

But this too hasty solution misses something essential, exactly what was strange in negation, 'its greatest point of gravity' (1993: 203): a sort of negative hunger, which Bataille inherits, and which he sharpens yet more, thus rekindling the anthropological sense of the whole undertaking. A burning impatience, 'involving all being,' forbids it 'ever stopping' (1993: 203) and thus completely changes the philosophical situation. Born directly of a disquiet that is only growing, the limit-experience will be the reverse side which the demand will lead to, when it becomes nocturnal and unfulfilled: 'the response that man encounters when he has decided to put himself radically in question' (1993: 203).

To explain this intensification, the necessity of which he vouches for, Blanchot in his turn adopts an ambivalent attitude toward the philosopher of Jena, between iconoclasm and legitimation. He first notes the key moments of Spirit, the diurnal side of a development that would claim to lead to the end of History and the omnipotence of the Subject, as if he recognized, in his way, the loftiness of the Hegelian idea, that places man at the center of the cosmos, and makes of him the master of all knowledge:

> At bottom, man is already everything! He is so in his project, insofar as he is all the truth to come from that whole of the universe that holds only through him. (1993: 204)

One by one, Blanchot goes over Hegelianism's conquests, its all-embracing and triumphant point of view: the dialectic utopia chanting the final realization of all things possible; the accession to truth of universal man. In this movement toward the summits, there is of course the indifference of idealism: the will of Spirit wipes away the singular person and drowns the individual tragedy in the justice of the State (cf. Hegel 1991: § 258, pp. 275–281; 1975: 52). But this private disaster plays its part in a higher end: now reason alone governs the march of civilizations. 'Negating nature and negating himself as a natural being' (Blanchot 1993: 205), Hegel's hero is the sovereign god whom Kojève described, this figurehead looking down on the given, empowered by the dialectic revolution. Advancing beyond the limit, and even beyond his own limit,[1] he reaches an exemplary plenitude which is 'conscious[ness] of the whole' (Blanchot 1993: 205), a tranquility without desire; divinely seated 'beside the river' (1993: 204), he has 'rejoined the point omega' (1993: 307).

But it is there, on this final chord, that the harmony will go awry, on this metaphor of the journey and of the goal attained. Indeed, with the *end of History*, it is an odyssey that reaches its conclusion, mechanically sustained right to its finish. Thought has gone 'through completely all [its] negations' (1993: 205); it has been able to oppose itself by every means, use up its critical power, '*transform into action, all [its] negativity*' (1993: 205, in italics in the text). It thus reaches the 'proud outcome' (1993: 204), giving us the image of a closed loop, of a space narrowed. The extreme now merges with the pattern of saturation: as if, for the absolute, there were no other possible milieu, no other means of epiphany, than that of closure.

---

[1] Cf. Hegel (2018: 38). 'But consciousness is for itself its own concept, thereby immediately the advance beyond what is limited and, since what is thus limited belongs to it, beyond itself.'

This eschatological perspective in which Blanchot fixes the German master allows him by the same token to shed light on the heart of the controversy. If Blanchot targets the Hegelian system at its apogee, it is doubtless in order all the better to decry its lethargy—the self-satisfaction, the resignation, the intolerable quietude. Of the initial negating drive there seems to finally remain none of the surge, no horizon: the future has been staked on this sole protestation, whose fervor has dried up. In its ascension toward hegemony, consciousness has found, at once, both its consecration and its point of no return: the passion of refusal is as if lightning struck in its brusque apotheosis. The future is sealed, the curtain falls. Gloriously eternal, man, crowned, is 'at rest in the becoming of his immobile totality' (1993: 205). Now awaiting nothing, he is prey to some internal Golem (1993: 203), as if petrified by an outcome that enervates him.

Blanchot sees no other means to escape the immobility, the 'closed circle' (1993: 207) of beatitude, than an infinite drift: to be faithful to unhappiness, wandering around on the outside, eluding capture. It is the very traveling of this route, this breathing in the open space, that must first be saved. So begins the retreat, an inversion of movement, before any signification; like an anonymous survival reflex, from the depths of this 'us' that bears human experience:

> But scarcely having said this [that man touches the absolute], we run up against this very assertion, as against the impossible *that throws us backward*. (1993: 205, our italics)

A marvelous image as of a balking horse, rearing up at the sudden brilliance of closure, and taking fright at the ataraxia of the end. Panicked by the final hurdle rising up before him, he withdraws, brought back into the 'not yet' of an active dynamic. Against this Parmenidian stiffening of the joints, Blanchot thus raises what he calls 'the decisive contestation' (1993: 205): a tide with no restraints, that crashes through the encirclement of the whole, and breaks down the walls around consciousness. 'No, man does not exhaust his negativity in action; no, he does not transform into power all the nothingness that he is' (1993: 205). For some sedition always remains left over that 'questions the infinite,' a furious negation that nothing can confine any longer, an unbridled impulse, which always breaks away, not satisfied with any respite, any achievement—even if this respite and achievement are magnified by metaphysics or by History.

Thought is thus radicalized, sets itself up as unpeaceable. It must, with no cowardice or half-measures, build up its revolt, go beyond Hegelian boldness, prove a willingness to go all the way, that is fully assumed and gratuitous: 'The limit-experience is the experience that awaits this ultimate man, the man who *one last time* is capable of not stopping at the sufficiency he has attained' (1993: 205, our italics). There is always something further, a *step-beyond*, a surplus to be brought into play: 'Perhaps [man] can reach the absolute by making himself equal to the whole [...]. But then *more extreme than this absolute* is the passion of negative thought' (1993: 205, our italics).

In a typical gesture, Blanchot here relies on what he plans to refute, as if to underline, as Bataille had done, his perverse—which is to say, inflexible, abyssal—fidelity to premises that he then immediately shelves. But if he first acknowledges the Hegelian ambition, its 'undeniable' and 'immoderate' character (1993: 208), he does so all the better to announce the difference, to reserve a place for the *ex-centricity* of a 'still more extreme' experience (1993: 208):

> This non-knowledge, said to communicate ecstasy, *in no way takes from knowledge its validity*, any more than non-sense [...] would turn us away from the active movement by which man tirelessly works to give himself meaning. On the contrary, let me insist again: it is only *beyond an achieved knowledge* [...] that non-knowledge offers itself as the fundamental exigency. (1993: 208, our italics)

The pattern which emerges for this reform is that of an overcoming. Following in Bataille's footsteps, Blanchot exacerbates the demand, does not renounce, never settles. He constructs his argument under the blazing sun of violence, in the rawness of an exigency without respite. Hegelian heroism is thus raised to incandescence, to that peak where Unity is overturned, where it is cut into and begins to flow through some unavoidable wound:

> interior experience [...] opens in this already achieved being an infinitesimal interstice by which all that is suddenly allows itself to be exceeded, deposed by an addition that escapes and goes beyond. (1993: 207)

There is therefore a 'surplus of emptiness' which haunts Hegelian plenitude, an impossible 'waiting for us behind all that we live' (1993: 207).

This 'surplus [...] of negativity' escapes from attempts to reduce it: somber and disoriented, the 'passion of thought' (1993: 207) rejects totalization, any recuperation by the system and even any substantialization of the 'nothing,' which would 'still receive from this ultimate negation a light' (1993: 208). Experience risks extreme subversion and transcends without 'reason': not in order to reach, nor only to infringe, but, like a force which goes on, spurred by an essential flaw.

The at once inexhaustible and imprecise character of this transgression is underlined by Blanchot, who takes care to arrive nowhere, at no place of refuge, to guard his journey from any implication of dialectic. It's an erratic, goalless wandering, which seeks only to lose its way, to go astray. The two orders of the circle and the straight line, of totality and infinity, here gloriously confront each other. On one side, the absolute—God, Being or Eternity—but this is only a stage on the way: man's truth is to cross over. Like Io, he goes beyond, in a disquiet attached to his being, which prevails over any enjoyment or any determination, which carries him away in its Heraclitean flow—the tip of an asymptotic breakthrough that opens onto the unknown. It pours out with an essential fluidity, evades the confines of the sphere and dispels any paralyzing mirage.

This breach is the mark of a constitutive insufficiency in man—at once instinctual and philosophical. Mixing here, in singular fashion, a formal logic and an affect, Blanchot clearly posits, at the ontological and psychic origin of what must be called a quest, an 'essential lack': an incompleteness born of completeness itself, an impulse unassuaged, which awakens in man an age-old questioning. This backward desire opens up an area of perpetual turbulence. One can sense here that nothing is ever finally established, that to each crest there corresponds a new emptiness, that the height itself is a hollowed-out abyss. One senses that man is reborn of this wound, on the other side of accomplishment. His unrest defines him, stamps with the seal of Pascal his anthropological difference. 'When the "doing" [...] is done, when, therefore, man has nothing left to *do*' (1993: 205, our italics), he can finally start to *exist*.

This transgressive existence is for Blanchot that of the Outside, of 'outside the whole' where one can spot the influence of Heidegger: the same collapse, the same abandonment to emptiness, through which the philosopher of finitude was already breaking the being-a-whole of beings. Being-ahead of oneself and the '*constant unfinished quality*' (Heidegger 1996: §46 p. 219 [236]) are the existential markers of a necessary disquiet, already porous and always penetrated. Some ten years after *Being and*

Time, the 'unemployed negativity' that Bataille identifies,[2] and which Blanchot rallies to without restriction, will deepen this gulf of *Dasein*,[3] this acquiescence in the fall, its aberrancy. The excess in refusal, what it supposes in terms of absolute dispossession, is now colored in funereal tones, following Heidegger's example. Death is the very name of this lightness, of this surge that breaks the circle and makes, from the voyage, an ever greater impossibility (Heidegger 1996: §53 p. 242 [262]); it is the dissipation of frontiers, a dive into a free and de-realized immensity. One senses here in Blanchot, as everywhere else in these texts, the dark blue trembling, the nomad joy of loss, where death must take over. Experiences follow and melt into each other, without any break in continuity. The '*capacity for dying*' (Blanchot 1993: 206, our italics) now expresses in terms of the infinite the 'radical negation' that no longer has an object, the eruptive dissatisfaction which 'has nothing more to negate' (1993: 205).

Through death, man cracks and is diluted, bearing his intimate devastation; he unravels and is annihilated toward his 'ownmost potentiality-for-being' (Heidegger 1996: §41 p. 178 [191]). Negation has been transmuted; it has become '*excess* of death' (Blanchot 1993: 206, our italics), suspended for an instant at the moment of sinking. Nonetheless, the emptying that Blanchot entrusts himself to does not really constitute a 'possibility' in the Heideggerian sense of the term. If the writer subscribes to this tutelary influence, it is in order to roll out his own—more weighty, more subdued—symbolic: death is condensed, becomes a theme in itself, piled up at its own frontiers, as if in the imminence of a threshold never crossed. One might say, at a push, that Blanchot here reads Heidegger literally, as Bataille had done with the Hegelian dialectic. If, at each instant, *Dasein* already exists *as finite* (cf. Heidegger 1996: §65 p. 303 [329], our italics), if it already exists 'authentically and totally,' already 'the being that it can be when "thrown into death"' (1996: §65 p. 303 [329], our italics)—it is because passing is not an event, but an accompaniment, a shadow, always on the heels of existence. It is not the outcome, but a form of being, a corrosion that gnaws at life with its monotonous nothingness. It is this state of slow osmosis that fixes the critic's attention and becomes for him the true space of an exploration. He works on testing it, unfolds it

---

[2] The expression is from Georges Bataille, in his 'Letter to X,' dated December 6, 1937 (1997b: 296). The author adds: 'I would not be able to define myself more precisely.'

[3] The term is understood in an anthropological, not its orthodox, sense, but in keeping with the theme of the analysis.

in a metaphorical and vagabond sense, before folding it back into the domain of lived experience.

But under these variations of Heideggerian being-for-death, one can hear, more muffled, Blanchot's reply to the Hegelian aporia. If the meaning of man only becomes clear in the vicinity of death, how can one live this death *most closely?* In a secondary and more hidden manner, it is the double obligation 'to be and not to be' that controls the process of Blanchot's reasoning here. Death in excess is then interpreted as the inability to cross over, like a *no man's land,* a median, passive, condition, between living and ceasing. We are, of course, very far here from the heroic tones of Kojève. But, in his more subdued manner, Maurice Blanchot rediscovers the oxymoron of 'living while dying,' its asymptotic tension at the margins of our fate. By Blanchot's account, '[b]etween being and nothingness,' the living death, the lived death, the foreseen torments of destruction, open the path of 'sovereignty' (Blanchot 1993: 209) magisterially glorified by Bataille, but which Blanchot's exegesis endorses in stranger terms than Bataille's, more exquisitely troubled at the vertiginous limit. 'Presence without anything being present,' thought without thinking, the neutral has become, in Blanchot's writing, the emblem of the impossible mediation, the 'between-the-two' into which to sink and lose oneself. An atonal and white life, already expunged from within, drowned in the ennui of the real. It is there that he stands, in the inexhaustible interstice, there that he touches the 'being without being,' of a colorless existence, the 'becoming without end of a death impossible to die' (1993: 209).

The writer places 'to live' within inverted commas (1993: 207), as if to indicate that other side, the lining of the days, 'that escapes all employ' (1993: 207), that passion of *not* which wears us out. Reticence before the end, in the interval that narrows toward the infinite, the refusal to arrive where our desire balks, compels us to a sterile patience, reduced to itself, reinvested for the sake of inactivity—an 'unemployable vacancy' (1993: 206), which remains suspended, only passively borne: 'As possibility, death gives *Dasein* nothing to "be actualized," and nothing which itself could *be* as something real' (Heidegger 1996: §53 p. 242 [p. 262]). More than a vow of indetermination, Blanchot understands in the words of the master an incitement to passivity. Having death in front of one, the running-ahead-of-death, implies giving up every point of 'support,' no longer being 'intent on something' (Heidegger 1996: §53 p. 242 [p. 262]). To surrender to circumstance, without 'imagining' any future, without expectation of any effect, to let oneself be overwhelmed 'by the infinity of the end' (Blanchot 1993: 206). The Heideggerian repugnance for 'bringing about one's own demise,' or even for 'dwell[ing] near the end,' lambasts those attitudes that still indicate a 'calculating' will (Heidegger 1996: §53 p. 241 [p. 261]), the concern to anticipate or subjugate death. For to open oneself up to the final possibility is precisely to give in, to yield blindly to drift, to being swept along toward the impossible that grabs us. One must no longer control, but 'let oneself be taken,' no longer 'producing' but 'spending,' to enter, by some mystical abdication (Blanchot 1993: 206[4]), the frozen exile of *worklessness.*

At the same time that it meets the requirements of thought, the attitude of this side of the frontier—at once death and epiphany—thus generates its own code of values. Under the species of the useless, Blanchot extends the anthropological reflection of his predecessors: the pattern of the unfinished curve, of that which necessarily sinks in the sands, calls, as if by an internal logic, he thinks, for an ethic of dis-interest. To not end amounts to no longer wanting, no longer being able, to desisting from oneself in a concerted abnegation, a relinquishing of all accomplishment. One finds again the imperative of aimlessness which we saw in Bataille, but in more pained tones, more in tune with the morass of our lives. On the edge of the argument, a 'situation' (Blanchot 1993: 210) is to be borne, the annihilation of all individuality, of all that which, in us, would have wanted to control and hold. Given over to chance, the self is dismantled, an 'I-who-dies' (1993: 209) and *experiences itself dying*, establishing itself through an unceasing defeat.

This paradoxical consent, no doubt, corresponds to what Blanchot meant by 'affirmation' (1993: 209): no longer the contesting of a truth, but ignorance, an amniotic environment, like a slow submersion. On the edges of the unthinkable, only this precariousness, between desire and refusal, can meet the double postulation of being and nothingness. The affirmation that 'does nothing but affirm' (1993: 209) attests to an availability 'without hope and without knowledge,' to an 'experience of non-experience' (1993: 210) where the voyage sinks, where thought, turned against itself, is annihilated between its poles.

It's as if one hears, in this abstention behind the 'decisive Yes' (1993: 210), a distant echo of the 'active passivity' which the great mystics of the

---

[4] Note that on the very same page Blanchot warns against the attractions of the mystical.

seventeenth century demanded of the soul, in its striving toward dispossession[5]:

> The height of passivity 'is that it becomes *passively active*, which is to say that it be as supple in all the actions that God will give it as it has been in all inaction, in all privation, in all suspension, or all suffering which God has placed it in, even to death.' (Le Brun 2002: 189, our italics)[6]

'Non-willingness' (Le Brun 2002: 185–186), the absence of will, like Blanchotian ataraxia, is not tranquil: it is not 'inaction' (cf. Fénelon 1983b: 1024), but rather pertains to the numbing of a hidden turbulence, some violent passion suffocated by its own excess, and which is paralyzed by its 'willing self-sacrifice' (Madame Guyon, cited in Le Brun 2002: 146). Fénelon thus carefully distinguished between the 'holy indifference'[7] of a soul 'equally ready to will and not to will,' and more placid 'indolence,' where is reflected, from the depths of the psyche, only a state of 'perpetual equilibrium' (Fénelon 1983b: 1024). Blanchot, in transposing this, will inscribe the same demarcation, preferring the man 'without horizon,' the only one who is able to live the limit-experience (1993: 210), to the man 'without need,' dolefully withdrawn into 'his immobile totality' (1993: 205). Although arising from opposite reasons, there are thus families of sensibility which give voice to the same shipwreck, to the same infatuation with dereliction. Negation does not mean lethargy, but a route, a being torn between death and life, a 'deadening' that is 'not yet a death' (Madame Guyon cited in Le Brun 2002: 185), but wherein already death has insinuated itself.

With Blanchot seems to grow clearer that part of quietism which was hidden under modern passivity, the Augustinian resonance of this letting-be and this abandonment. Like a vow of solitude, a vow of extreme deprivation, which would have 'relegated and deposed the world of values' (Blanchot 1993: 209)—a non-substantial ego, this 'particle of dust' (1993: 209), as the great masters of uncompromising spirituality described

---

[5] I can only refer the reader here to the wonderful book by Jacques Le Brun (2002: 187 and 189).

[6] The author is here citing a letter by Fénelon (1972: 122). In the same passage, Le Brun makes explicit reference to Blanchot's essay on Bataille: 'These are perhaps the best ways to say today, by way of oxymoron, what passivity and inaction said in the seventeenth century' (2002: 190).

[7] The expression is from Saint François de Sales (Le Brun 2002: 161).

themselves. Pure love 'claims nothing, [...] expects nothing, [...] desires nothing' (Madame Guyon cited in Le Brun 2002: 159). It wears down all willing, all reality, ousting the person as singular identity. 'As if love were pure once the subject broke away from it, absented herself from it, and as if this love without a subject now turned to its object and, so to speak, were absorbed into it' (Le Brun 2002: 161).

One senses, in this abdication without reserve and this resolute blandness, something like a ritual oblation. Pure love has this sacrificial ambiguity, this absoluteness of obliteration[8] which turns into joy. A *potlatch* of the forces of life, of all instinct, of all utilitarian calculation. It 'destroys with a strange impetuosity'; it tears out the hope of being at the very root. Pure love 'hates itself' and 'makes its pleasure from its pain' (Madame Guyon, cited in Le Brun 2002: 147), raising anonymity to the level of voluptuous pleasure. Thus, the man of Blanchot 'in some sense already belong[s] to this detour' (Blanchot 1993: 210); he has always been a wandering and a dispersion. Given over to the night, he accepts the abrasion of experience: not a night of stars, which would offer a response, in its 'vanishing immensity,' but 'the *other* night,[9] false, vain, eternally restless (Blanchot 1993: 210). His only hope is frustration, his desire, desire for the 'infinite lack' (1993: 210), for what only happens in withdrawal. His exaltation arises when he is lost, as if by a joyous collapse, in which is confirmed the ruinous nature of the enterprise. Without any 'promise' or 'recompense' (cf. Fénelon 1983a: 661–662)[10] without anything remaining to which one

---

[8] 'Pure love [...] is a priest who is never without sacrifice, and who is never satisfied until he has stripped away everything: I say EVERYTHING without exception [...]' (Madame Guyon, cited in Le Brun 2002: 159).

[9] Marlène Zarader makes night, understood in Blanchot's sense, the focal point of current philosophy:

> If Blanchot shares with many of his contemporaries the will to do the night justice, and if he supposes, as they do, that this justice will only be done by a thought at least open to an 'otherwise than being,' he is, doubtless, the one who has best judged what this openness will require, the one above all, who has sought to consummate the sacrifice: to be done with being, and the security it offers, to renounce *meaning* itself. (2001: 33)

[10] Fénelon here makes the *impossible supposition* 'that God wanted to annihilate [his] soul at the moment when it detached itself from [his] body' (1983a: 661). 'Allowing these very possible suppositions, there is no more promise, either of recompense, or of beatitude, or of hope in a future life' (1983a: 662).

might cling, with which to delude oneself, through which to overcome the exquisite uniformity of unhappiness.

This life 'between two deaths,'[11] willingly compressed within insipidity, bundled up 'behind the door,'[12] which, of becoming, keeps only the bloodless face, is nonetheless not abstract, not a pure product of speculation. In order to live as one dies, says Blanchot,[13] to shake up the cinders of meaning, one need only trust the sensory: the unnumberable and cyclopean being of immediate impression, the profuse disorder—'massive, absurd, [...] absolutely singular' (Marquet 2009: 40)—that reveals to us Hegelian 'certainty.'[14] One need only return to that which 'is' (Blanchot 1993: 33), to the dark and disappearing 'earthly body' (1993: 37), to the 'strangeness of this singular end' (1993: 35). Reality is then perceived 'even unto death' (1993: 37); it 'is' only to become corrupt, no longer luxuriating and gorged like that of Bataille, but charred, chaotic and barren. Evoking Plato's *Sophist* (1993: 35) and the question of being, Blanchot recalls in this regard that there is a way to know 'the shattering of chaos' (1993: 37), that of relying on matter—in its raw sense of enigma, in its sense of bitter dissolution. Matter in its strangeness, as cadaver and putrefaction, infesting life; when nature appears as carrion,[15] opaque in its very meaninglessness, impersonal and decimated.

This 'banality' of the world (1993: 35), this 'immediate that defeats every grasp' (Heidegger, commenting on Hölderlin, cited in Blanchot 1993: 37), marks also the only outcome, the absolute poverty that allows the consciousness to approach the real face to face, as Hegel thought concerning death. Blanchot here follows Bataille, as if to express in the one breath with him, under 'the black star-filled sky,' the presence analogous

---

[11] We will meet this expression of Lacan's again in the next chapter, which deals with his work.

[12] From the Wolfgang Borchert play *Draussen vor der Tür*, 1947.

[13] The end of this chapter draws on an earlier essay by Blanchot, taken from the same collection: 'The great refusal' (Blanchot 1993: 33–49).

[14] Cf. G.W.F. Hegel's *Phenomenology of the Spirit* Chap. A, 1: 'Sensory certainty: the This and my view of the This'. [Translator's note: *La certitude sensible ou le ceci et ma visée du ceci.* This was Jean Hyppolite's translation (Hegel 1966) of Hegel's '*Die sinnliche Gewissheit oder das Diese und das Meinen.*' Hyppolite in his translation aimed to underscore the subjective dimension in this first form of consciousness, expressed in Hegel's substantivized verb '*Meinen*' (think/mean/intend). Hegel (2018: 43) translates the phrase as 'Sensory Certainty: The This and Meaning.']

[15] Cf. Blanchot (1993: 37). 'the Sacred is "immediate" presence. It is this body that passes, is pursued and nearly grasped even unto death by Baudelaire.'

to loss, the 'silence of lightning' and the 'towering flight' (Bataille 1988: 18[16]) of existing: 'exceeding and excluding any present,' presence is always ecstasy, impossible encounter, it tears given reality into the pieces of an 'infinite absence' (Blanchot 1993: 38).

By dint of antitheses, the combined discourse of the two men thus marks off an affirmative zone, a patient gleaning at the frontiers, like an enclave of being in the land of nothingness. Sensory life, by virtue of its dispersion, its 'flow[ing] in slow rivers through the inky sky' (Bataille 1988: 18), offers a 'possible substitute to death'[17] a 'that' where decomposition is directly felt, a prolonged 'stay' with the intolerable, that part of dread hidden behind the singular and furtive occasions: 'I don't see anything: *that* is neither visible nor sensory. *That* makes you sad and heavy from not dying' (Bataille 1988: 32[18]).

This raw experience, more desolate than death, this poetic suffocation is not the sole purview of the poet; nor is it limited to the universe of Blanchot, whose meditation, throughout his works, echoes a whole series of fraternal voices: Bonnefoy, Baudelaire, Hölderlin, Char. One must also mention especially the work of Levinas, so close in this point to Blanchot's perception, and what Levinas calls 'nakedness of being' (Levinas 2004: 90).[19] Under the label of the *there is*, transposed from Heidegger,[20] Levinas seeks to express the 'impersonal, anonymous, yet inextinguishable "burning" of being' (Levinas 2004: 93–94). An unceasing 'murmur' (Levinas 2004: 94–95) that does not well up from the pit, but from life with its impenetrable face, from shared existence that flows and persists 'even in its annihilation' (2004: 100). Between life and death, 'there is' represents this 'excluded middle' (2004: 38) that death does not resolve, this pure 'fact of existing' (Levinas 1987: 47), that imposes itself and finds its kingdom *on this side of the limit*. A 'field of forces' (1987: 46) that is not nothingness (cf. Levinas 2004: 94), but silence in excess, the rumbling that one hears when one puts an 'empty shell' close to the ear (Levinas 1985: 48). '[I]mpersonal like "it is raining" or "it is hot"' (Levinas 1987: 47), the

[16] [Translator's note: I have departed here from the translation in Bataille (1988).]
[17] 'To me this world, the planet, the starry sky are just a grave' (Bataille 1988: 12).
[18] [Translator's note: I have departed here from the translation in Bataille (1988).]
[19] Levinas himself cites the relationship between this concept of his and the Blanchotian neutral: 'It is a theme I have found in Maurice Blanchot, even though he does not speak of the "there is" but of the "neutral" or the "outside"' (Levinas 1985: 49).
[20] 'There is [*Il y a*]' translates the German '*Es gibt.*' Cf. Heidegger (1990: 197). 'We do not say: "Being is," "time is"—but "there is Being," and "there is time."'

void exhales its abundance, in the very place 'where the bottom has fallen out of everything;' the ego is abolished in its turn and perishes in the flow that submerges it. 'Like [an] unreal, invented city' (Levinas 2004: 97), where one would wander, in the threat of pure presence, in the astounding vacillation of familiar things.

Faced with the same burden, Levinas seems to agree with Blanchot in expressing in his way the cadaver, the chaos or matter (Levinas 2004: 100, 97, 91–92). Both come to the edges of the Nothing to delve into this extreme form of presence represented by the 'absence of everything' (Levinas 1987: 46)—when the irremissibility, the monotonous superfluousness, of existence shows itself. It is this anguish before Being, more original, perhaps, than that before death, that Levinas will try, however, throughout his entire œuvre, to overcome. He stands before the world, accepts its *thirst and hunger*, seeks therein a path of freedom: the possibility one can glimpse, of breaking away from the anonymous never-ending roll of waves, the emergence of a subject, who reestablishes the instant and breaks up the invasion of the obscure (cf. Levinas 2004: 69, 109–113, 139–141). Years later, the author would confirm, and amplify, this choice of 'resistance'[21]:

> In fact, this idea was only a first stage […] *responsibility for the Other*, being-for-the-other, seemed to me, as early as that time, *to stop the anonymous and senseless rumbling of being*. It is in this form of such a relation that the deliverance from the 'there is' appeared to me. (Levinas 1985: 51–52, our italics)

There is nothing like this in Blanchot.[22] The awful flirtation with the elementary seems to fill the entire field, letting no light filter through, with no other adventure bar entrapment and stunned shock. Nonetheless, this submergence, this allegiance to a time without redemption, does not in the end exclude the opening up of a chink. Blanchot's *Infinite Conversation* is beset, as one sees on rereading, by the always-vain attempt to come to terms head on, in its paradox, with the *double* face of the real: this *immediate* which nonetheless 'allows no mediation,' this *so-close* in which one can feel, precisely, 'infinite separation' (Blanchot 1993: 45). Like an 'other dimension' (1993: 45) attached to the quotidian, a sudden alterity incised

---

[21] '[…] that resistance against anonymous and fateful being' (Levinas 2004: 80).

[22] It is in this sense that Levinas himself comments on Blanchot: 'It seems that for him it is impossible to escape from this maddening, obsessive situation' (1985: 50).

into every obvious object, every familiar impression. In this Mobius strip that enwraps us, the relationship with naked presence and the unthinkable in this relationship are witness also to 'our most human belonging to immediate human life' (1993: 47). It is in contact with 'the incessant' (1993: 45) and 'the neutral' (1993: 47), in contact with this originary experience which precedes all affirmation (cf. 1993: 47), that impossibility 'becomes alluring and takes form' (1993: 48), that it reveals itself as desire.

This is when speech offers an opening. In order to thus stay in 'the diverging of difference' (1993: 46), in order to implant this 'presence to which one cannot be present' (1993: 45), in order to feel that which 'escapes our power to undergo it' (1993: 45), an awakening is needed: that of an other response, born of the elusive, heralding—in 'communication' or poem—the very dimension of impossibility (cf. 1993: 48).[23]

Only language, in effect, seems capable of eluding the actualizing force of the world and its surge toward the known (cf. 1993: 40–41), only speech born of vertigo, fallen from an 'other region' (1993: 47), could take on this task. Only 'inspired words' (1993: 68) could reveal the obscure 'in its obscurity' (1993: 44), could signify the Outside in its intimacy, and presence as dispersal. Like the prisoner in the fabled cave, who wants to get behind the fire, and spots his own shadow as he turns away from it.   '

This would be a disavowed language, dedicated to the immediate, which would be the only language able to extract from an indistinct sensation 'this unique now, [...] the proper enigma of what dissolves there' (1993: 34). It would be suited to resolving this very torment, as it surfaces in the opening pages of *The Phenomenology of Spirit*, against the grain of its entire later argument. Not without sadness had Hegel accepted the sacrifice of the singular experience, that one must 'miss the *this*' (Marquet 2009: 44), which evaporates in the very attempt to describe it:

> Now; it has already ceased to be when it is pointed out. The *Now* that is, is another Now than the one pointed out, and we see that the Now is just this: already to be no more when it is. (Hegel 2018: 46, our italics)

---

[23] Marlène Zarader (2001: 17) underlines the exemplary character of Blanchot's efforts in this also: 'Up until not so long ago, philosophy's ambition was to grasp that which is, to align itself as closely as possible with all presence. Today, it wants to accept that which hides, to approach the abyss, to attest to that which is fated to escape it.'

This man of nostalgia, sensitive to the violence of the word in the eva-nescence of the impression,[24] had nonetheless opted for a more certain solution, better adapted to the aspirations of consciousness. After Hegel, but in a different way, Blanchot goes back to the same nub: to the mythical place where the fruits of the night offer themselves in withdrawing, to the dark side of the moon, which unveils itself in the instant that it disappears.

The final word goes thus to writing: not only to live as one dies, but to 'recapture' presence as that which has faded, to 'miss' the 'broken leaf of ivy' (Blanchot 1993: 34), the better to express it; to take up again the paradox at its source, at the point of crisis where it is seen that the word erodes that which it names, that there is no language without destruction.

What seems to fascinate Blanchot is precisely this murder that lies within designation, that acts as a key. The disintegration of the object, corollary of every expression, is perhaps, in fact, the only way to *live* extinction, to endure the ephemeral. To recite the sensory as it hides, to hold the disappearing essence of the immediate: that which 'is,' in the sense of that which dies. The poem thus replays, in ritual fashion, the nec-essary abolition of the visible, the process of its dissolution. Even more than it bears witness, speech *accomplishes*, it sacrifices the real in pronounc-ing it; through this consuming, it *realizes* the erosion that forms the 'ulti-mate dimension' (1993: 48) and the dying heart of our life.

In order to give back to life its mortal resplendence, one need only reach that which precedes the word, its leaven of instability and ruin. Blanchot still believes in the epic of the Letter, doomed to eternal failure. To go down into the Underworld, to bring back Eurydice: it is always a collapse toward speech, a call to desolation. It is death itself, with its scent of springtime, it is dead life itself that Blanchot goes in search of in the Underworld, magnified by its prohibition. This priestess function of lan-guage, when desire no longer tends to save, but to lose, to become loss itself, merged with its sign; this vocation of obliteration, in the manner, confusedly, of Bataille, is that of poetry, of what Blanchot calls poetry—which is to say, a kind of speech that 'says' nothing, but which, eager for the unknown, 'simply answers' (1993: 48), 'aggravat[ing] instead of resolving' (1993: 41),[25] attentive to that which invariably turns away.

---

[24] 'In the actual attempt to say it [the bit of paper], it would therefore rot away' (Hegel 2018: 48).

[25] Blanchot cites here the epigraph to Yves Bonnefoy's collection of essays *L'Improbable* (cf. Bonnefoy 1983).

For the intention is not to achieve a work of art, but to grasp the essence 'where it appears,' to touch it 'at the heart of the night' (Blanchot 1982: 170). Eurydice twice lost in the instant that she reveals herself, when the artist turns to look at her. And yet, how can one not turn toward her? How can one not, by dint of one's very demand, ruin all hope of meeting her 'in her nocturnal obscurity, in her distance, with her closed body and sealed face' (1982: 171)? The writer lingers over this phantasmal embrace, at the boundaries that thought dreams. Eurydice, recognized in her very invisibility, coveted as that foreignness that 'excludes all intimacy' (1982: 171). Eurydice, whose name summons up that aporia, that false transcendence which racks life, that *transimmanence*[26] which must be conquered and laid bare—not in order to 'make her live,' but, says the legend, in order to 'have living in her the plenitude of her death' (Blanchot 1982: 171). Plenitude-death, embraced as a dawn, as an immense body where desire would swoon, where it succumbs and is fulfilled.

BIBLIOGRAPHY

Bataille, Georges. 1988. *Guilty.* Trans. B. Boone. Venice Beach, CA: Lapis.

———. 1997a. Hegel, Death and Sacrifice. Trans. J. Strauss. In *The Bataille Reader*, ed. F. Botting and S. Wilson, 279–295. London: Blackwell.

———. 1997b. Letter to X, Lecturer on Hegel. In *The Bataille Reader*, ed. F. Botting and S. Wilson, 296–300. London: Blackwell.

Blanchot, Maurice. 1982. *The Space of Literature.* Trans. A. Smock. Lincoln: University of Nebraska Press.

———. 1993. *The Infinite Conversation.* Trans. S. Hanson. Minneapolis and London: University of Minnesota Press.

Bonnefoy, Yves. 1983. *L'Improbable et autres essais.* Paris: Gallimard.

Fénelon, François. 1972. *Correspondance.* Éd. Jean Orcibal. Paris: Klincksieck.

———. 1983a. Lettres et Opuscules spirituels XXIII. In *Œuvres I*, ed. Jacques Le Brun. Paris: Gallimard.

———. 1983b. Explication des maximes des saints sur la vie intérieure. In *Œuvres* t. 1, ed. J. Le Brun. Paris: Gallimard.

Hegel, G.W.F. 1966. *Phénoménologie de l'Esprit.* Trans. J. Hyppolite. Paris: Aubier-Montaigne.

———. 1975. *Lectures on the Philosophy of World History: Introduction: Reason in History.* Trans. H.B. Nisbet. Cambridge: Cambridge University Press.

---

[26] The expression is from Jean-Luc Nancy (1997: 56).

———. 1991. *Elements of the Philosophy of Right*. Trans. H.B. Nisbet. Cambridge: Cambridge University Press.

———. 2018. *The Phenomenology of Spirit*. Trans. M. Inwood. Oxford: Oxford University Press.

Heidegger, Martin. 1990. *Questions III et IV*. Paris: Gallimard.

———. 1996. *Being and Time*. Trans. J. Stambaugh. New York: SUNY Press.

Le Brun, Jacques. 2002. *Le Pur Amour de Platon à Lacan*. Paris: Seuil.

Levinas, Emmanuel. 1985. *Ethics and Infinity: Conversations with Philippe Nemo*. Trans. R.A. Cohen. Pittsburgh: Duquesne University Press.

———. 1987. *Time and the Other, and Additional Essays*. Trans. R.A. Cohen. Pittsburgh: Duquesne University Press.

———. 2004. *De l'existence à l'existant*. Paris: Vrin.

Marquet, Jean-François. 2009. *Leçons sur la Phénoménologie de l'esprit de Hegel*. Paris: Ellipses.

Nancy, Jean-Luc. 1997. *The Sense of the World*. Trans. J.S. Librett. Minneapolis: University of Minnesota Press.

Zarader, Marlène. 2001. *L'Être et le neutre: A partir de Maurice Blanchot*. Paris: Verdier.

CHAPTER 6

Beyond *Atè*: *Jacques Lacan*

Abstract We discuss Lacan's thought in his seminar on *Ethics*, which ties in indirectly to the Hegelian thematic. The distinction which he draws between pleasure and *jouissance*, that is, between the morality of modera-tion and the passion of the incommensurable, allows him to trace in his turn this extreme frontier, 'that human life can only briefly cross.' Like Blanchot, Lacan imagines a between-two-deaths, where man's ethical sense meets the aims of his desire. This is exactly where Antigone stands, an exemplary and fascinating figure, haunted by 'going beyond.'

Keywords Antigone • Ethics • *Ding (das)* • The thing • Signifier • Between-two • *Jouissance*

Published after his death, Jacques Lacan's course on *The Ethics of Psychoanalysis* ran from autumn 1959 to summer 1960. It marks a turning point in the history of his thought, when Lacan begins to explore the margins of the semiotic 'reason' that was dominant at the time. From the end of the 1950s, he begins to plot a configuration that is more porous,

---

From the ancient Greek *Aτη*, which means at once fault and fate (from the name of the goddess Atè, goddess of error and confusion, of *hubris*): 'It is an irreplaceable word. It designates the limit that human life can only briefly cross' (Lacan 1992: 262–263).

B. Rojtman, *The Fascination with Death in Contemporary French Thought*, https://doi.org/10.1007/978-3-030-47322-8_6

open to transgression and to otherness; his reflection grows to take in the field of the unthought, of a beyond-of-the-signified (Lacan 1992: 54) that escapes the totalizing grip of the system: which Lacan will name the Real.[1] His approach thus overlaps with the post-Hegelian problematic of the limit. Nor should one be surprised that, in these post-war years, still marked by Kojévian anthropology, this limit would take on an existential and radical coloring, that of the division between life and death.

Indeed, beyond the analytic work proper, it is the general question of what is man that is posed here, that of the meaning of the human, throughout a long, subtly complex text, that concludes, at the end of the study, with the figure of Antigone, an Antigone more fascinating, more solitary than ever, caught between obliteration and regret, but who looks death face to face, from deep within her cave; already dead and living, like all the heroes of her type, like the sentinels already imagined by Kojève or Bataille. And this is indeed the question asked by the 'Preface' to the *Phenomenology*, to know what happens, at the frontier of being, to the meaning that is distilled of our life, when it comes down to the instant of pure risk. What happens at that dividing line where our value system, hastily constructed from an ordinary existence, topples over completely and gives way before the unknown? What does it mean, for man, this confrontation with the ultimate, where one's life, as it capsizes, necessarily goes outside of itself? At that boundary where nothing else matters but one's singularity as human being, and—Lacan will say—one's very *jouissance*?

Thus retranslated, Lacan's point of departure in his reflections becomes congruent with the presuppositions of philosophy. 'The function of the pleasure principle,' writes Lacan, 'is to make man always search for what he has to find again, but which he never will attain' (Lacan 1992: 68). One can hear, in the paradox formula, the echo of that 'lack' of being which Blanchot spoke of (Blanchot 1993: 205) and which sets man on a pursuit without respite. It is still the same primordial demand, but now transposed into a dynamic of the affects, where desire has taken the place of negation, and the pleasure principle, that of dialectical reason.

Like Blanchot, Lacan divides the space of the quest into two areas, which refer to two registers of desire. The first is subject to the symbolic order, where the pleasure principle dominates. The second transcends these limits; here, instinct breaks the barrier of signs and throws the subject toward his or her *jouissance*. It marks the crossing of a line, toward

[1] I would like to acknowledge here my debt to Susana Huler in my initiation into the thought of Jacques Lacan.

some blinding, dazzling center which, throughout the text, will be called *das Ding* or *the Thing*. This diptychal, hierarchical structure, thus, from the start, places at the center of these reflections what Blanchot, following Bataille, called *the limit-experience*: at the edges of the possible, an unexplored region, a subversive breakthrough that surpasses the quotidian and leads to the inconceivable.

A thought of the threshold and of infraction: Lacan addresses the question of pleasure from the angle of balance. He subsumes its modalities under 'the law of that which functions *on this side*' (Lacan 1992: 246, our italics[2]). In keeping with the Freudian approach, he emphasizes its essentially regulatory character: that which allows the maintaining of libidinal energy within the limits of nervous tolerance, below the critical level of excitation which the psychic apparatus can bear (cf. 1992: 222). 'The outer extremity of pleasure is unbearable to us to the degree that it involves forcing access to the Thing'[3] (1992: 80[4]).

It is from this perspective that Lacan addresses Freud's *Entwurf* or *Project* (Freud 1895/1950), where one can already perceive this temperance which constitutes the deep law, and, in a way, the very possibility, of pleasure: 'The originality of the *Entwurf*,' for him, 'resides in the notion of path-breaking [*frayage*] that controls the distribution of libidinal investments in such a way that *a certain level, beyond which the degree of excitation is unbearable for the subject, is never exceeded*' (Lacan 1992: 222, our italics[5]). In these prolegomena to Freudian thought, path-breaking is conceived as a path of 'facility' [*facilité*] (Lacan 1992: 222), and pleasure, as an outflow or 'discharge' (1992: 27). It is always a question of going toward the most comfortable, toward that which eases, of serving a basic tendency to 'inertia' (1992: 19), thus avoiding the choppy waters of excess:

> The pleasure principle governs the search for the object and imposes the detours which *maintain the distance in relation to its end*. (1992: 58, our italics)

---

[2] [Translator's note: I have departed here from the translation in Lacan (1992).]

[3] While explicitly basing his analysis on Freud, Lacan, throughout this discussion, will echo Heidegger's questioning of the traditional concept of Thing: beyond its function as object, the thing *as thing* draws back from apprehension. Its *thingness* 'remains concealed, forgotten' (cf. Heidegger's essay 'The Thing': 2001: 166–168).

[4] [Translator's note: I have departed here from the translation in Lacan (1992).]

[5] [Translator's note: I have departed here from the translation in Lacan (1992). '*Frayage*' is Lacan's term for Freud's '*Bahnung*,' which Lacan says is wrongly translated into English with the term 'facilitation' (Lacan 1986: 49 and Lacan 1992: 39).]

In the spirit of Freud, the pleasure principle thus has a value of *mediation* between the 'exigencies of life' (*Not des Lebens*[6]) and the 'the outer extremity of pleasure' (1992: 80). Like dialectic, his 'scientific psychology' seems to trace, *on this side* of that extremity, the axes of a general 'economy' which forms a buffer, implanting its logic and its modes of functioning. This organization in system form arranges the constellated movement of representations around a foreign term—the object, the Thing (cf. 1992: 58). In keeping with his times, Lacan translates this Freudian construction in terms of *semiosis*: 'In Freud,' he notes, 'the characteristic of pleasure [...] is to be found on the side of the fictitious,' which is to say, 'precisely what I call the symbolic' (Lacan 1992: 12). And it is 'the return of a sign' (1992: 12) that man hopes for when, 'subjected to [...] the pleasure principle,' he enters the labyrinth of signifiers (cf. Lacan 1992: 134).

Thus caught in the nets of language, desire is dulled and distracted, following a rationality which, while regulating energy displacements,[7] at the same time inhibits them.[8] The plastic, substitutive, nature of this network, 'commits human libido to [...] slipping into the play of signs (1992: 91[9]), without ever transcending it. Borne 'from signifier to signifier' (1992: 119) in circular pursuit and wandering, desire stays 'at as low a level as possible' (1992: 119), knocking against the symbol like a bee against the window-pane; it goes astray in the mirror of tropes, in this fluid web where representatives are infinitely exchanged and approximate[10]—while it continues to be magnetized, from afar, by some 'formidable center that sucks [it] in' (1992: 246).

[6] The expression is taken directly from Freud (1895/1950: 297).

[7] Cf. Freud (1895/1950: 296): 'neuronal excitation as quantity in a state of flow.'

[8] Cf. Freud: 'neurones tend to divest themselves of [quantity] Q' (principle of inertia) (Freud 1895/1950: 296). And, on endogenous stimuli (principle of constancy): 'the nervous system is obliged to abandon its original trend to inertia [...] Nevertheless, the manner in which it does this shows that the same trend persists, modified into an endeavour at least to keep the [level] as low as possible and to guard against any increase of it, that is, to keep it constant' (Freud 1895/1950: 297).

[9] [Translator's note: I have departed here from the translation in Lacan (1992).]

[10] Cf. Lacan 1992: 58: 'In this orientation to the object, the regulation of the web, the *Vorstellungen* relate to each other in accordance with the laws of a memory organization, a memory complex, a *Bahnung*, i.e. a path-breaking, [...] whose operations the neuronic apparatus perhaps allows us to glimpse in a material form, and whose functioning is governed by the law of the pleasure principle.' [Translator's note: I have departed here from the translation in Lacan (1992).]

This amalgam of the codes of pleasure and of representation allows Lacan to extend the argument to the whole of human *praxis*. The spider's 'web' where man is trapped indeed delineates all psychic and political activity of the polity. It engages the meaning of the human and its values, which is to say, the ethical ends toward which tend 'every art and every inquiry' (cf. Aristotle 2011, 1094a 1)—and even psychoanalysis itself. This expansion to anthropology gives the question of the limit, of moderation through pleasure, its true scope.

In the first part of the seminar, where the axiological correlates of desire are examined, as our cultural history has collected them, Lacan chooses therefore to place himself under the authority of Aristotle: he follows him in underlining, at the base of human behavior, the 'enigmatic' convergence of happiness and the good.[11] If pleasure, in effect, 'appears in many cases to be [...] in opposition to moral effort' (Lacan 1992: 36), this tension is resolved in the principle—or rather is absorbed in the, postulated, inverse merging—of 'just action' and 'joy': 'actions in accord with virtue,' says the philosopher, 'would, in themselves, be pleasant' (Aristotle 2011, 1099a 23–24). Morality thus remains the 'ultimate point of reference' (Lacan 1992: 36) by which the hedonism that is dominant in our civilization regulates itself—but on the condition that this morality remain prophylactic, 'concerned with pleasures and pains' (Aristotle 2011, 1104b 16).[12] In this alignment with the psychic, the idea of the Good is inseparable from its connotations of 'well-being' and of 'goods,' in a pluralized use that underscores the inadequacy of virtue alone in grounding the authority of ethics:

> It [happiness] manifestly requires external *goods* [...] For it is impossible or not easy for someone without resources to do *what is good*. (Aristotle 2011, 1099a 32–1099b 1, our italics)[13]

Jacques Lacan can thus conclude:

> [F]rom the origin of moral philosophy, from the moment when the term ethics acquired [...] meaning [...], all meditation on man's good has taken

---

[11] Cf. Aristotle 2011, 1095a 15–19: 'let us state [...] what the highest of all the goods related to action is. As for its name, then, it is pretty much agreed on by most people: [...] it is happiness.'

[12] Cf. Aristotle 2011, Book X, which deals with pleasure and true happiness.

[13] [Translator's note: I have departed here from the translation in Aristotle (2011).]

place as a function of the index of pleasure. And I mean all, since Plato, certainly since Aristotle, and down through the Stoics, the Epicureans, and even through Christian thought itself in Saint Thomas Aquinas. (1992: 221)

Throughout the study, Lacan will play on these interferences, underlining the hybrid, somehow impure, character of a domesticated desire, where happiness and virtue concur.[14] This 'impurity' of the quest is due, in a certain manner, to its allegiance to the order of the sign: from its calculation-based parameters, its equilibrium between pleasure, judgment and reality, 'in harmony with reason' (Aristotle 2011, 1102b 28). In the kingdom of Logos, a certain restraint is required—arising from this evaluation itself, from this negotiation, this distribution of desires within the borders of the possible. A prelude to Freudian positions on pleasure, the ideal posited by Aristotle is nourished by temperance and proportionality:

Thus every knower of the excess and the deficiency avoids them, but seeks out the middle term and chooses this. (Aristotle 2011, 1106b 5)

Moral virtue [...] is a mean between two vices, the one relating to excess, the other to deficiency [...] aiming at the middle term in matters of passion and action. (2011, 1109a 20–24)

This is the morality therefore, of the *well-tempered*, of a life-wisdom adapted to circumstance, whose essential flaw, in Lacan's eyes, will be only its claim to cover the entirety of human hopes:

The leader is he who leads the community. He exists to promote the good of all. [...] His error of judgment [...] is to want to promote the good of all—and I don't mean the Supreme Good [...] but the law without limits, the sovereign law. (Lacan 1992: 258–259)[15]

For this is in fact only a first stage, a still traditional morality, '[concerned with the] *insofar as it is possible*' (Lacan 1992: 315, in italics in the

---

[14] Cf. Aristotle 2011, 1102a 5–6: 'happiness is a certain activity of soul in accord with complete virtue.'

[15] One can recognize the Hegelian opposition between 'human law' and 'divine law' (cf. Hegel 2018: §§448–449, p. 177). And see note 38.

[Translator's note: I have departed here from the translation in Lacan (1992).]

text). 'The cleaning up of desire, modesty, temperateness' (1992: 314)—
this morality of the golden mean 'is wholly founded on an order' (1992:
315) that guarantees civil life and the correct working of the polity. It
displays a dialectic superiority, perfection achieved, at the peak of a prag-
matic structure that respects hierarchies and is adapted to the public space.
It is a question of achieving, under the species of virtue, a good that is
'useful' and profitable to the greatest number, a good in which the citizen
who is respectful of the institution, the man of reason and discourse, gets
his rightful amount of pleasure.[16]

While presenting here, as Blanchot had done, a phase he recognizes as
necessary, Lacan nevertheless criticizes, behind this conciliatory philosophy, the pusillanimity of satiated polities, of closed off and uneventful soci-
eties, where Disorder has yet to show itself. He condemns an emasculated,
bourgeois morality—that of utilitarianism, a morality of vassals which will
not suffice, as he proposes to demonstrate to us, to quench the thirst of
princes.

Thus commingled with ethics, the pleasure principle shows itself more
than ever the principle of the *lesser evil*, intended above all to maintain the
cohesion of the system and to prevent any overflow. Lacan highlights this
effect of retreat by a continual return to the text of Freud's *Project*, where
an atmosphere of ebb tide dominates, the continual shadow of a degree
zero. Hemmed around with guard screens, with fenders against shock,
with discharge mechanisms, pleasure imposes its law, in the double sense
of the regulation of internal functioning and of protective barrier. Pleasure
remains confined to the orbit of the Good, which is to say, to our timid
game of *live-as-one-can*, to the domain of restraint and the ordinary. The
pinnacle that its calculation can aim to reach is invariance: a form of essential passivity, a lazy regulation of the forces that pull at us.[17] Of this serenity
that it imagines, our thought still masters the quiet dream. Its absolute is
one of languor, a nirvana where one reaches, not ecstasy, but the flaccid
finite, the satiety of a life blindfolded. Pleasure is prudent. It sails far from
the sirens' reefs and keeps to the bearable.

---

[16] Cf. Lacan 1992: 228, and its reference to the utilitarianism of Jeremy Bentham.

[17] We will not go into the terminological ambiguities that underlie the evolution of
Freudian thought. Lacan does not seem to want to distinguish between 'the originary tendency to inertia' and its modification by the 'exigencies of life' (cf. Freud 1895/1950: 297);
see the entries 'Principle of constancy' and 'Principle of inertia' in Laplanche and
Pontalis (1973).

One senses in these descriptions a hint of boredom, a sort of Lacanian disdain for what is already given, for that which is satisfied with what it is. For, says Lacan, 'Neither pleasure nor the organizing, unifying, erotic instincts of life suffice in any way to make of the living organism, of the necessities and needs of life, the center of psychic development' (1992: 104). This meager happiness, with its 'common approaches' (1992: 219), this 'short and well-trodden satisfaction,' (1992: 177) is disparaged by the poet in Lacan, who unmasks its alienating lure. One must reject the 'benevolent fraud of wanting-what's-best' (1992: 219[18]), one must pass the 'strong wall' that the good builds 'across the path of our desire' (1992: 230). There is an ideal of frugality to be overcome, a comfort to be left behind, in the perilous manner of the great tragic figures. The splendor of '*das Ding*,' at this magnetic point whither the '*Triebe*' stubbornly push us, has indeed 'nothing at all to do with something that may be satisfied by moderation—that moderation which soberly regulates a human being's relations with his fellow man at the different hierarchical levels of society' (1992: 110). Man's true desire is 'an incommensurable measure, an infinite measure' (1992: 316), that goes on its way without turning back. Haunted by some memory, some fantasmatic presence that has been taken away, like a mirage or a daze. Desire is like Parmenidian radicalism, which rejects all that which only *exists*—this radical desire which nothing pacifies, which nothing sates and which remains tormented with an irremediable 'want-to-be' (1992: 294).[19]

Like Blanchot, Lacan prefers the intense: a questioning without respite, that does not fear the extreme. A 'non-desire to cure' (1992: 219), which, undermining even the absolute, repudiating its wholeness, forces the circle of signifieds[20]—toward that which Lacan calls The Thing, and which does not have a name.

[18] [Translator's note: I have departed here from the translation in Lacan (1992).]

[19] [Translator' note: 'want-to-be' is the translation which Lacan suggested for the phrase '*manque-à-être*' (Lacan 2001: x).]

[20] Cf. Lacan 1992: 54: 'Das Ding is that which I will call the beyond-of-the-signified.' Contrary to Saussure, from whom he draws inspiration, Lacan disconnects the signifier from the signified and gives primacy to the former. In our context, while the double network of signifiers and signified remains subject to the law of pleasure, the Signifier, for its part, tends to become autonomous as letter or as image, emptying itself of all specific signification. At the extreme, it represents on its own the access to the Symbolic, which is to say, the break from the natural substrate and the distinctive mark of the human. Cf. *infra*, note 155.

In *Black Sun*, Julia Kristeva refers to these pages of Lacan while distancing herself from him. From her point of view, depression and melancholy are signs of the same '*signifier's*

In antithetical fashion, this gushing forth relies, again in the manner of Blanchot, on the very pleasure that it wants to *sublate*, on the painstakingly constructed sphere of wisdom and the Good—like a leap that breaks through the barrier of restraint, like a necessary deconstruction. For the good alone 'cannot reign over all without an excess emerging' with 'fatal consequences' (1992: 259). The settled order seems thus to give way from within, as a result of some ultimate interrogation, of some stubborn yearning for the abyss. As if, 'as soon as everything is organized around the power to do good, something completely enigmatic appear[ed] [...] to us [...] the ever-growing threat within us of a powerful demand whose consequences are unknown' (1992: 234).

It is this reactivation of the demand, this metonymic pursuit, that is polarized and 'oriented,' at the endless end of desire, by the strange magnetism of the Thing: an unnumberable and empty 'Outside,' a point of blinding glare that Lacan signals as 'the absolute Other of the subject' (1992: 52).

This theme of going beyond, of otherness as superior level, goes back to the originary experience of the *Nebenmensch* (caregiver[21]), that grounds our relation with the Other and our 'first apprehension of reality' (1992: 51). The analyst returns to Freud's understanding of the infant's indistinct perception of a vital presence, that of the helpful stranger who has come to end the infant's distress—a presence at once identifiable and unknown, analogous to himself and also radically distinct. More than the experience of satisfaction properly speaking, Lacan's exegesis accentuates the ambiguous division between the familiar and the inaccessible, where is powerfully expressed 'the beside yet alike, separation and identity' (1992: 51). 'Thus the complex of the [*Nebenmensch*]' as Freud understands it 'falls apart into two components': one can be 'understood' from former impressions, the other is completely 'new and *non-comparable*' (Freud 1895/1950: 331, our italics).[22]

---

failure' (Kristeva 1987: 10). The Lacanian *Thing*, on the other hand, although it is 'beyond-of-the-signified,' remains a 'word'; it continues to ground, even if in enigmatic and 'mute' form (1987: 14), the constitution of the subject and the omnipotence of the Signifier.

[21] [Translator's note: 'caregiver' is my translation for '*prochain secourable*,' which is the standard French translation for the German '*Nebenmensch*.' The English of the *Standard Edition* of Freud's works translates it as 'fellow human being.']

[22] Out of concern for exactitude, Lacan translates the phrase from Freud cited here (1992: 51).

Lacan retains the dichotomy and projects it onto the universe of representations. That which, in Freudian terms, refers to the 'understanding,' for him falls within the symbolic order and pleasure' regulations. But this order itself must be negated, transcended by a strange and 'wild' surplus. Beyond the 'ψ system' and the 'earliest *Vorstellungen*,' there is '*Das Ding*'—which is '*something entirely different*' (Lacan 1992: 52, our italics).

Which is to say, firstly, something incommensurable: that which one cannot approach, which one cannot account for. This Real of which Lacan makes a vaguely sensed externality, a presence without form. It is the hidden face of the *Nebenmensch*, which 'makes an impression by its constant structure and stays together as a *thing*' (Freud 1895/1950: 331 in italics in the text).[23] By definition, it is impenetrable, expelled to the other side of the gates of signification. Something being-there, outside the law, with an indecipherable aura, 'entirely different' from the inventory of the describable attributes of the object. *Das Ding* is without remainder, without function, without representation: the lost object that was never there and will never be found again. It offers itself only by its trace; for 'one doesn't find it, but only its pleasurable associations' (Lacan 1992: 52).

This indirect refraction, which at least allows one to spot some glimmer of the unrepresentable, is the oblique way to address the anonymous: the Thing, at the end of the day, will always be 'represented by emptiness, precisely because it cannot be represented by anything else—or, more exactly, because it can only be represented by something else' (1992: 129–130). A Heideggerian vessel or jug,[24] a box of matches on the collector's mantelpiece,[25] emptiness as such hides, allows itself be sensed only through the form that encloses it. The ordinary object, as soon as its use value is taken from it, exhibits its mute neutrality and offers itself to the gaze. It becomes empty indication, now 'gratuitous, proliferating, superfluous' (1992: 114). Its 'thingness' reveals itself in this pure exposition, in the suspending of its finality and the absurdity of its sole presence. For Lacan as for Bataille, the utilitarian and signification are equally servile and riveted to this side of the frontier. Going beyond this limit, the empty boxes threaded together are laid out in arabesques, sovereign in their

---

[23] This is also directly translated by Lacan (1992: 51).

[24] Cf. *supra*, note 111.

[25] Lacan recounts seeing a collection of such boxes at the home of his friend Jacques Prévert (1992: 114).

enigmatic givenness—which is still not the Thing, but allows us taste its unfathomability.

This first theorization of the real, enriched by new references, will little by little take a more disquieting turn. The reference back to the same childhood experience, but this time as Freud describes it in his 1925 essay 'Negation,' adds to the test of judgment—which was initially essentially cognitive—a value of affect. For if the exteriority of the *Nebenmensch* allows the child, guided by the happy memory of the attentions he received, a progressive adjustment to reality, the 'outside' of the negation, on the other hand, is from now on determined as a space of rejection: it becomes the melting pot of the impressions vomited out by the ego, the field of denial and of the excluded. Now, exteriority will be perceived as bad, in the sense of a suffering without content, a pure evil, inherent in the 'elsewhere.'[26]

The overlap of texts thus allows the psychoanalyst to mingle the strangeness of the *Nebenmensch*—the strangeness of the helpful person, of the wonderful happiness of the flesh, of the presentiment of the ungraspable—with a pernicious 'outside,' doomed to ostracism and rejection. This moment seems decisive for the rest of the seminar: using the ambiguity of the Freudian formulations, Lacan combines the unknown, the extra-territoriality of the non-symbolic, of that which 'remains together as a thing'—with this menacing strangeness, beyond the system, where everything gathers which the ego, who wanted to live, has fled and condemned. But inversely, this referral of the external to the shadowy figure of the *Nebenmensch* establishes an element of *interiority*, which will remain curiously attached to the 'strange.' If that presence alongside us (*Neben/à côté*), despite the fuzziness of its contours, is felt as something tender and familiar, the disqualified and pushed outside Other will conserve, in his turn, some feature of that first intimacy:

---

[26] Cf. Freud (1925/1961: 237): 'the original pleasure-ego wants to introject into itself everything that is good and to eject from itself everything that is bad. What is bad, what is alien to the ego, and what is external are, to begin with, identical.'

It is in 'Instincts and their Vicissitudes' (1915/1957) that this learning of the real takes on a negative coloring, the subject-object opposition (ego-external world) becoming correlative to the opposition pleasure-displeasure (cf. 'Pleasure-Ego/Reality-Ego' in Laplanche and Pontalis 1973).

> Much that he [the individual] wishes to eject because it torments him yet
> proves to be *inseparable from the ego*, arising from an inner source. (Freud
> 1930/1961, p. 5, our italics)

In a remarkable interweaving, Jacques Lacan thus slips in, with the cita-
tions from Freud's 'Project' or his 'Negation,' formulations from others of
Freud's essays that clarify the process of expulsion while confirming the
interior origin of the banished element (see Freud 1915/1957: 135).

Setting aside the nuances peculiar to each context, Lacan brings to light
the recurrence of a function. It is by a wrenching, by a certain violence
against oneself, that this radical exterior is established—which is refractory
to all meaning[27] and, precisely, which knows no other determination but
that of referring back to the lost interiority. The exterior is interiority's
blurred reflection at the highpoint of difference, interiority's paradoxical
image: at once *Nebenmensch* and execrable, monstrous and cherished.
One could say that '*das Ding* is at the center only *in the sense that it is
excluded*' (Lacan 1992: 71, our italics). It is 'the prehistoric Other that it
is impossible to forget—the Other whose primacy of position Freud
affirms […], something strange to me, although it is at the heart of me'
(1992: 71). A black hole at its most distant, and yet the very essence, the
very heart, of our ontological reality. What Lacan will call, in a flamboyant
phrase, 'extimacy' (1992: 167).

The question of the Real thus opens in a tragedy. It begins with an
ontological loss, anterior to any object, with an insurmountable fracture,
constitutive of our identity, the pain of which is born with our life. This
'*Fremde*, strange and even hostile on occasion' is also 'that around which
the whole progress of the subject is oriented' (1992: 52[28]). The *Fremde*,
the stranger, is the archaic and absent kin, forever essentially correlated
with our being, toward whom our desire turns, toward whom it makes its
lamentation and its plaints, in order all the better to be disappointed.

A passion for the most distant that summons us by its very proximity, a
necessarily frustrated expectation of something *alongside* us but necessarily
kept at a distance. Phantasm of the Mother, of the Other as self. Stubbornly
fixated on the Thing, burning and unfulfilled, the sunflower-like-desire is
called to be reborn, like the phoenix. In its impulse toward no object, it

---

[27] Cf. Lacan 1992: 52: 'an outside which, Freud tells us, has nothing to do with that reality
in which the subject will subsequently have to locate the *Qualitätszeichen* [signs of quality].'

[28] [Translator's note: I have departed here from the translation in Lacan (1992).]

merges with 'change as such,' becomes in itself 'the metonymy of the discourse of demand' (1992: 293). Going from one illusion to the other, it can only wear itself out, toward some incestuous ecstasy:

> The step taken by Freud at the level of the pleasure principle is to show us that there is no Sovereign Good—that the Sovereign Good, which is *das Ding, which is the mother, is also the object of incest, is a forbidden good, and that there is no other good.* (1992: 70, our italics)

The *Nebenmensch* complex thus responds to the post-modern necessity of always reiterating the demand. It gives a name to the want-to-be, offering its psychic models as a way to express this infinite process—with only this modification, that what was 'passion of negative thought,' pursued beyond the perfect,[29] here takes on an instinctual coloring. Pleasure leads us to the limits of the livable, to the foot of an invisible wall where it destroys itself. One must there choose between crossing over and normality. Whether to leave the symbolic, which is reason—but also falsehood and domestication by signs. One must choose whether to hallucinate even further in the name of some radical absolute, which captivates us in its mirages. Caught in the trap of the aporia, where the human condition is maddened to exasperation, authentic desire, as Lacan understands it, now rejoins the posture of the Kojévian hero, left alone in the face of the unbearable.

In Lacanian terms, this vertiginous border line is that of *jouissance*: 'beyond the pleasure principle,' a panicked, harmful experience, that is attempted only on the edge of the abyss. An experience that coincides with the Hegelian function of the 'negative' which Spirit must face, with the 'absolute disintegration' through which Spirit achieves its truth (cf. Hegel 2018: 16).

For if we see 'the subject retreat from his own *jouissance*' (Lacan 1992: 194), and 'start to weaken when the first half-serious step is taken' toward it (1992: 185), it is because *jouissance* implies an element of 'intolerable cruelty' (1992: 194). To explain this contradiction, Lacan turns to another facet of Freudian thought, whose unspoken elements he recomposes. He detects there a new form of love—more savage, basic, less controlled. The

---

[29] Cf. Blanchot 1993: 207: 'Thus, at present, the problem brought forth by the limit-experience is the following: how can the absolute (in the form of totality) still be gotten beyond?'

jouissance that operates there shines, beyond pleasure, with a disquieting luster; it partakes of a perverse satisfaction where the *love of one's neighbor* is realized, insofar as this love contains the constitutive evil that inhabits the human heart, and its 'unfathomable aggressiveness':

> Men are not gentle, friendly creatures wishing for love, who simply defend themselves if they are attacked, [...] a powerful measure of desire for aggression has to be reckoned as part of their instinctual endowment. (Freud 1930/1961: 69)

Love of one's fellow man appears now as only the civilized mask of an intractable aversion. *Hate your fellow man as you do yourself* becomes once more the fundamental directive—insofar as you resemble him, hate him to the measure of his own hatred: subject to the same instincts, to the same desire to do harm.[30] In a mirror effect that is somewhat Hegelian, the subject quickly recognizes in himself the violence detected in the other—this execration which he must protect himself against, certainly as victim, but just as much as perpetrator: *jouissance* has entered the realm of the Thing, whose threatening 'extimacy' it reflects. The evil it implies turns back like a wounded beast, goes back to the origin, folds over and doubles, merging the sufferings, infinitely reflecting the need to destroy:

> My neighbor possesses all the evil Freud speaks about, but it is no different from the evil I retreat from in myself. To love him, to love him as myself, is necessarily to move toward some cruelty. His or mine? [...] [N]othing indicates they are distinct. (Lacan 1992: 198)

Under the identification with the other's barbarity, under the *jouissance* of evil, something new quickly becomes obvious, something ever murkier: it is not just through fear of virtue, through a general awareness of our own cruelty, that man retreats before the love of his neighbor, but because this merciless aggressiveness overlaps, more covertly, with a suicidal attraction, like an instinct toward annihilation. The need to lay waste is only the recognizable emergence of a latent, archaic tendency toward self-destruction. In the course of his reflections, the father of psychoanalysis

---

[30] Maimonides interprets the legislative intention of *Leviticus* 19, 18 as an injunction to love one's neighbor 'as you love yourself.' In our context, the strict observance of the commandment would thus imply that one hate the other 'as much as you hate yourself' (*Séfer Hamitzvot, Mitzvot Assé* 206).

looks deeper into the machinery of this tendency, which is complex but of capital importance:

> It was not easy, however, to demonstrate the working of this hypothetical death instinct. The manifestations of Eros were conspicuous and audible enough; one might assume that the death instinct worked silently within the organism towards its disintegration, but that, of course, was no proof. The idea that part of the instinct *became directed towards the outer world and then showed itself as an instinct of aggression and destruction* carried us a step further. (Freud 1930/1961: 78, our italics)[31]

Not graspable directly, the death instinct can only be perceived through a mask: the visible screen of hatred,[32] the palpable and composite exteriorization of an internal need for sacrifice, which expresses itself only in this form. The true, sacrificial and funereal, end of desire, looms behind its warlike face, still mingled with Eros, who at once both hides and shows this sacrificial goal.[33]

This camouflage explains, it seems, Freud's repugnance for any consideration of universal love, an unjustifiable and measureless love of the Other. If the author of *Civilization and Its Discontents* unambiguously admits his reticence—'Why should we do this [love our neighbor]? What good is it to us?' (Freud 1930/1961: 65)—it is doubtless, suggests Lacan, because the love at issue here, this extravagant, unreasonable love, is exactly that which falls within the scope of *jouissance*: beyond pleasure, a malign and unregulated voluptuousness, a corrupting love that clasps its

---

[31] In the Preface to the French edition (Freud 1930/2000: xiii), Jacques André comments on the evolution of Freud's position on this point. As he sees it, the 'displacement of the internal to the external' marks a regression 'compared to the bold ideas of 1920.' Lacan, for his part, will bring the death instinct back to its original interiority, which is to say, its self-destructive roots.

[32] This perception by transparency can be compared with the Dionysian appearance, as Nietzsche analyzes it in *The Birth of Tragedy*. 'Even the brightest clarity of the image [seemed] to conceal something as much as it revealed it' (Nietzsche 1999: §24 p. 112).

[33] Cf. Freud 1930/2000: 81: 'it [the death instinct] eludes us wherever it is not betrayed by a fusion with Eros.' One could already find, underlying *Beyond the Pleasure Principle*, the intertwining of the contradictory principles of life and death. The instincts almost seemed to function according to one sole regressive model: 'They [sexual instincts] are *conservative* in the same sense as the other instincts in that they *bring back earlier states* of living substance' (Freud 1920/1961: 34, our italics).

object to it all the better to cause its ruin; born of an archaic instinctual source, it carries with it, concealed within in, the nourishing shade of death.

To go beyond, to transcend toward *jouissance*, is thus to go into oneself in unhappiness and desolation. One can then understand that we are held back by a reflex of horror, which expresses the instinctive 'resistance' (Lacan 1992: 194) of the ego before the chasm. But this dyke itself gives rise to new waves. The barrier of meaning, of existence and of fear will be broken by an impulse of the entire being, an anarchic revolt that topples the mediocre and pulverizes its lawfulness. For the infinite can emerge only through some form of violation.

This dialectic of excess, in order to be triggered, relies on the 'strong wall' (1992: 230) that blocks its horizon. A double bind of limit and dissipation; the Law is required, Lacan will say, to ground the probability, and even the very desire, of transgression:

> Is the Law the Thing? Certainly not. Yet I can only know of the Thing by means of the Law. In effect, I would not have had the idea to covet it if the Law hadn't said: 'Thou shalt not covet it.' (1992: 83)[34]

The obstacle is transformed into catalyst, whipping up passion, making it 'flare up' (1992: 101) in fervor. The *sublation* of pleasure reaches its true dimensions, its tragic extravagance, only on the basis of this Interdict, which reveals the saturnine meaning of desire, how much it contains of taste for death—at once Greek and Pauline, sin and *hamartia*. Desire without mediation is 'radically destructive' (1992: 283), necessarily incendiary and guilty. The dyke is only there, as sentry of destiny, to push the hero toward his mortal fate.

In the faltering of dread, crossing the bar,[35] the Lacanian hero achieves his freedom. He renounces the natural order, the established forms of institution and power, in order to better lose himself in 'turmoil' (1992, 249[36]). In a *corps à corps* with evil, a confrontation with a 'faceless fate,' he affirms his 'power' (1992: 195) by this very risk. His path is one of great

[34] Lacan is here knowingly transposing Saint Paul's words on the relationship of law and sin: 'I had not known sin but by the law: for I had not known lust except the law had said, Thou shalt not covet' (*Romans* 7:7).

[35] [Translator's note: '*franchissant la passe*': this is a phrase coined from the maritime metaphor of passing the channel at the mouth of the port. Obviously, I turned to Tennyson for a suitable translation.]

[36] [Translator's note: I have departed here from the translation in Lacan (1992).]

storms: summoned by the abyss, he walks toward the other side of all life, toward the death in all life. His daemon destines him for some superior disaster.

In this consenting to 'pay the price' (1992: 321), Lacan bolsters his own ethics of overcoming. As the seminar progresses, he turns away from Aristotle and adopts a more Kantian point of view. He will find there the force of torment, a valorization of pain, a righteousness in harm undergone, which affirm suffering as sole horizon, as sole correlate of the effort of will:

> In brief, Kant is of the same opinion as Sade. For in order to reach *das Ding* absolutely, to open the floodgates of desire, what does Sade show us on the horizon? In essence, pain. (1992: 80)

If desire and ethics are, then, once again placed on the *same* side of action—it is the side, this time, of excess; with the same effort required of both, the acceptance of the same danger. What there is in the Kantian *Thou shalt* of hungered, feverish and exhilarating, is revealed precisely thanks to this conflation. Lacan emphasizes its intransigence, its heroic grandeur. He lays bare the affects that permeate and invigorate *practical reason*, the folly of a rigor 'that nothing on earth satisfies' (1992: 316). For 'the moral imperative is not concerned with what may or may not be done' (1992: 315). It throws wide open the doors of the unconditioned: the will is 'altogether independent of the law of appearances' and of any 'law of causality' (Kant 1997, AK 5: 29). A song of liberty that celebrates the impossible, where is laid out the secret 'topology of our desire' (Lacan 1992: 315), where reason and instinct intertwine in the one famine. A song of a lordly virtue which is indifferent to that which is, which abandons the mediocrity of pleasure, and gives of itself to the point of self-annihilation.

Mystical, haughty, as if still colored with a pietistic austerity, this disinterest[37] seems to prepare the way for the contemporary negativism: a sovereign morality, freed of any mooring in nature, of any calculation, of all miserable necessity; a fierce, conspicuous rupture with the needs of life, with that which the animal in us cries out for: well-being, happiness, the indulgence of instinct. One can hear, in this tragic insolence, very close to

---

[37] Cf. Lacan, on Kant: 'For it to be valorized as the properly ethical field, none of our interests must be in any way involved' (1992: 315).

the post-Kojévian sensibility, an *apologia for the useless*, for which Kant has become the inspired preacher:

> Either there is no higher faculty of desire at all or else *pure reason* must be practical of itself and alone, that is, [...] *without presupposing any feeling* [...] *without any representation of the agreeable or disagreeable*. (Kant 1997 AK 5: 24, our italics)

A disdain for subordination, for what gets consumed, what is stored up in the name of survival. Hence the *potlatch* (Lacan 1992: 235): it has, like desire, the splendor of ceremonies of initiation, of those sacrilegious feasts which give access to the brotherhood of masters, to the shared authority of an obscure contempt.

By routes different from Kant's, but by a logic that accords with his secret impulse, Lacan underlines the difficult cost of this advance toward unbreathable heights. Less idealist, less disembodied than philosophy, psychoanalysis follows every step of this rebellion that has risen from finitude, its mortal and dolorous meaning: what it means to renounce the flesh, the clarity of pleasure and of the happy medium; what it costs to aspire to the immense, forgetting the 'pathological interests' that hold man back and check him, on the 'risky path' (1992: 323) of his lightning-struck shock.

The fiery glow of the fall: Lacan will give it its full poetic power in his epilogue. Antigone is the name of the admirable obstinacy,[38] this pride 'unyielding right to the end, demanding everything, giving up nothing, absolutely unreconciled' (1992: 310).[39] Antigone, insatiable and aflame, who 'assume[s] the crime' (1992: 283) right to the end, and goes imperturbably into an 'engagement with annihilation' (1992: 309–310). Her

---

[38] This choice is of course no accident. Lacan is following the path laid down by Kojève and Hegel. Moreover, the entire nineteenth century celebrated Sophocles' *Antigone* and the 'celestial' figure of its heroine. Georges Steiner endeavors to analyze the reasons for this privileged status, without managing to make them completely clear: 'Complete answers elude us. Only the judgment of supremacy is clear. From it arise some of the most radically transformative interpretations ever elicited by a literary text' (Steiner 1996: 19). For Hegel, the relationship of brother and sister marks the highest degree of natural ethical consciousness. Guarantor of the divine law, the sister tragically opposes the human law of the state: 'The loss of the brother is therefore irreparable to the sister and her duty towards him is the highest' (Hegel 2018: §457 p. 181). Kojève comments on this famous section of Chapter VI in his 1935–1936 course (cf. Kojève 1997: 98–107). Jacques Derrida, in his turn, will offer a reading of the chapter in *Glas* (cf. Derrida 1986: 163ff.).

[39] The passages cited (1992: 309–310) refer, in Lacan's text, to the character of Oedipus.

unflagging and unmediated path takes up the entire final section of the book; it brings with it something of that metallic passion that grips us with her coruscating implacability. It allows us to see what happens 'beyond the barrier' (1992: 232), at that 'limit' (1992: 272) where the Sophoclean hero steps forward and chooses to be mortal, 'after having gouged out his own eyes' (1992: 309[40]):

> [...] *rather not to be.*
>
> That's the choice with which a human existence, such as Oedipus's, has to end. It ends so perfectly that he doesn't die like everybody else, that is to say accidentally; he dies from a true death in which he erases his own being. The malediction is freely accepted [...] of the subtraction of himself from the order of the world. (1992: 306, italics in the text[41])

The tone is certainly one of philosophical Romanticism, a sort of glorious Jansenism, where all the worldly values of nation and love are expunged. There is nothing left but to be, at the end of all these voids which we bear within us. Antigone is the figure of outrage, at once victim and exterminating angel, who, alone, remains, beyond *Atè*. Standing on these reefs, beyond this line 'that human life can only briefly cross' (Lacan 1992: 262–263), she accepts the final combat. Summoned to this crossing, this margin, on some martyr's rock where she is exposed, suspended at this edge, subsisting while suffering.

It is there that the author will look for his heroine, it is there that he places her, in the space of this infinite, Borgesian, time, that separates the leaving of the world of the living from annihilation itself. Like the thinkers who preceded him, Lacan takes up his character as she stands between two worlds, 'between two deaths' he says (1992: 270), in the moment of passage—which Antigone's walling up in the cave expresses metaphorically, and extends. A bird frozen in full flight, Niobe changed to stone, the young girl knows that she is dying, eternally held at the edge, eternally fated to the 'secret miracle' (cf. Borges 1998) of imminence: 'the meaning of the situation or fate of a life that is about to turn into certain death, a death lived by anticipation, a death that crosses over into the sphere of life, a life that moves into the realm of death' (Lacan 1992: 248). An

[40] [Translator's note: I have departed here from the translation in Lacan (1992).]
[41] [Translator's note: I have department here from the translation in Lacan (1992).]

asymptotic zone, 'as total darkness approaches,' where nature totters and 'changes aspect' (1992: 264[42]); an undecided zone, in the anonymous 'between-two' where existence flags, drawn to the cataclysm, where it drops toward its extinction.

From one session of his seminar to the next, Lacan readjusts his definitions. Whether he's joining death to life, or a first death to the 'second death' (1992: 285[43]), the 'between-two' is a concept in itself, independent of where it is applied: from existence to being, from being to nothingness, it is always the same gap, it is the distance as such that makes meaning. One can recognize, in this 'divinization [...] of the limit' (1992: 262), a ghastly response to the Hegelian aporia. Antigone's between-two-deaths, an 'exemplary image'[44] of the death without death of the Kojévians, sinisterly crystallizes the dream of Blanchot or of Bataille. But from 'that limit where her life is already lost' (1992: 280), caught in the glue of her own consciousness, the daughter of Oedipus can at last consider her youth and weep for it. Antigone, suspended between consciousness and collapse, turns toward the instant of revelation—sufficiently to live it, to be and to die at once, persisting and crucified, in these long death throes that only tragedy can capture:

When does this [Antigone's] complaint begin? From the moment when she crosses the entrance to the zone between life and death [...] Although she is not yet dead, she is eliminated from the world of the living. And it is from that moment on that her complaint begins, her lamentation on life. (1992: 280)

The between-two is a region of the consciousness, a fundamental ennobling, where is confirmed the 'being-for-death' of the hero. It is in this stasis, a moment torn from the chasm, that the essential becomes visible: not only man's desire, in his impenetrability, but his very life, at last addressed and recognized, from this far away exile, at last 'lived and thought about' (1992: 280), in the moment of the syncope it will sink

[42] [Translator's note: I have department here from the translation in Lacan (1992).]

[43] The idea of a 'second death' is suggested to Lacan by a passage in Sade's *Juliette*, which Lacan cites at length: 'To be of even greater service to nature, one should seek to prevent the regeneration of the body that we bury. Murder only takes the first life of the individual whom we strike down; we should also seek to take his second life' (1992: 211).

[44] 'The exemplary image which attracts to itself all the threads of our desire, the image of the crucifixion' (Lacan 1992: 261–262).

into. Like the perishable immediate, life disappears in the moment one thinks it—or like the *broken leaf of ivy* which Yves Bonnefoy sought to describe in its evanescence and which, in memory, traces only a fragile erosion (cited in Blanchot 1993: 205).

At this frontier where everything totters and everything appears, spirit is petrified in its own debacle, but sustained by some astounding flash that transfixes it. It has nothing more to do, except to endure and to see, caught in the gap between worlds, stunned by 'an essential blindness' (1992: 281). Lacan translates the unbearable of this 'space of freedom' (1992: 261), 'the violent illumination' (1992: 281) at the crossing of the *Atè*, by recourse to the aesthetic. For only beauty can encompass this supreme overturning, where the meaning of our destiny is in play, at once suffocation and overexcitement of thought; only this phosphorescence allows an intuition of it, a fleeting unveiling of 'I don't know what mystery which could not be articulated up until now,' which 'forces you to close your eyes at the very moment you look at it' (1992: 247[45]):

> [...] it being precisely the function of the beautiful to reveal to us the site of man's relationship to his own death, and to reveal it to us only in a blinding flash. (1992: 295)

Lacan can't say enough about the immaterial grace of the young girl, which arises from her resistance and indeterminacy. She has the magnificence of heroism in vain, the 'latent, fundamental' radiance, which the analyst tells us belongs already to our collective unconscious, which he says 'forms part of [our] morality' (1992: 284). Nailed to the spot, outside of the 'limits of the human' (1992: 263), at the center of tragedy, Antigone refracts onto us her own fascination. Between blindness and rapture, she stands in the breach, sole and solemn for an instant, facing the funereal sun. Lacan ponders the 'dissipatory power of this central image relative to all the others that suddenly seem to descend upon it and disappear' (1992: 248). As if, from this sepulchral blaze, one were to retain only the elegance, one were to approach it only through the majesty of a *scene*. For *jouissance* is spectacle: it has the powerlessness, the seduction of the useless, of that which leads to nothing, except to this pyre where desire *surrenders*, finds in annihilation its fulfillment. Desire comes to fruition on

---

[45] [Translator's note: I have departed here from the translation in Lacan (1992).]

the sacrificial altar toward which tends the long human saga, in this meta-physical and cruel theater where our imaginary is purged.

Since Kojève, no one had so well expressed the 'humanist' meaning of this wedding feast, its pride in perdition, this privilege of nothingness that distinguishes man from all living species, and blissfully offers him up to the knife. In some magnificent passages, the psychoanalyst—the poet—pays tribute to Antigone's resolve, her testimony as dead young girl, her truth greater than existence, which ultimately pushes 'the human adventure [...] through to its end' (1992: 309).

But the daughter of Oedipus is not content to unfold before us her sacral ritual, however transgressive and bewitching it might be. She also leaves us, as testament, at the end of her harsh mission, her charred Word. Free of any biological tie, Antigone brings to language the will that animates her, her protest of a thinking reed. The death instinct, by which is illumined her most deeply buried truth, wrests her away from the earthly ground. Consenting to her temporal condition, she makes shine, above immediate contingency, the splendor of the 'Signifier.'[46] The passion that pushes the young girl into nothingness has, as has been said, nothing to do with any 'Nirvana [...] principle,' or any 'fundamental law [...] of universal equilibrium' (1992: 211).[47] Rather, she bears witness to the endless caesura which is imparted to the sensory continuum by the negativity of spirit: that is, a power of separation, of abstraction from the given real, whence begins the History of men. Of this 'activity of the Understanding,' in the style of Kojève,[48] of this castrating initiation, the Signifier is the warrant—which constructs a sovereign universe, rising out of the sands, its arches anchored in the void. The Signifier is the sole preserve of man who leans on nothingness, the begetting of the Subject, which presupposes 'somewhere—though certainly *outside of the natural world*—that *which is the beyond* of that chain, the *ex nihilo* on which it is founded and articulated as such' (1992: 212, our italics).[49]

This obligatory point of rupture, this 'hole' that is found out 'at the center of the real' (1992: 121), is not only the vertigo of the abyss, which

---

[46] Cf. *supra*, note 128.

[47] The psychoanalyst returns untiringly to the distinction to be drawn between 'the tendency to return' and 'the death drive' (which is in the historical domain) (cf. Lacan 1992: 211).

[48] Cf. Kojève 1973: 127.

[49] Or also, further on: 'Without the signifier at the beginning, it is impossible for the drive to be articulated as historical' (Lacan 1992: 213.)

haunts the Sophoclean hero; despite everything that recurs, in the Lacanian pattern of themes, related to the chasm and the extreme limit, here the negative takes on, explicitly, its active value; it grounds the 'point of view of an absolute beginning,' of a radically 'distinct' anthropological 'order' (1992: 213–214). This 'creationist' dimension[50] seems in the end to prevail over death, to explain its ontological seductiveness: the 'will to destruction' (1992: 212) is only the obverse of an expectation that is deeper, more bereft, but no less fevered: the impatience for 'an Other-thing' (1992: 212), for a dawn, that opens '*from zero*' (1992: 212, our italics).

As if death were hiding life. As if the desire for death were the shy face of man's mad pride, and of his royalty. Taking up the ancient claim in new terms, Lacan seems to add his voice to the Kantian call for autonomy. But in a more eager fashion, more absolute, inherited from Hegel: in that desperate manner that separates the human from the material chaff, at the risk of saving him from it by unhappiness. One must pay 'with a pound of flesh' (1992: 322) one's entry into the Symbol; one must buy with one's life this preeminence, this solitude of a dispossessed king.

Death is a scarification, an initiatory passage—in order to be reborn to the transfigured universe of the sign. In order to be reborn to prophetic meaning, without content, without object; to the coronation through language, in its fluidity, before any signification; between concreteness and nothingness, to this mirage of pure designation, of levitation above bodies. The Signifier is a consecration, a germination of what subsists when presence is crucified. It goes right to the unthinkable: to that which, outside the system, manifests itself only as indefeasible opacity. At this summit where life, stripped of its trappings, of its superfluities, of its existential tocsins, becomes again a precious gem, an essence, what remains when all has been lost. 'A pure and simple relationship of the human being to that of which he miraculously happens to be the bearer, namely, the signifying cut that confers on him the indomitable power of being what he is in the face of everything that may oppose him' (1992: 282).

Such is the law proper to Antigone, such is her privilege at the moment of the tomb. At the moment without reason where is revealed her supreme ego, her 'has been,' the 'mysterious and profoundly obscure fact of having

---

[50] Cf. Kojève 1973: 116: 'human Reality [...] exists only as a creative movement.'

lived'[51]—at the moment when there floats, alone, naked and disembodied, the simple statement of a Name:

> My brother may be whatever you say he is, a criminal. He wanted to destroy the walls of his city [...] but he is nevertheless what he is [...] As far as I am concerned, the order that you dare refer me to doesn't mean anything, for from my point of view, my brother is my brother [...] My brother is what he is, and it's because he is what he is and only he can be what he is, that I move forward toward the fatal limit. (1992: 278–279)[52]

The Signifier prevails over all determination. It is even the opposite of the signified. It lays waste to meaning, to everything that accords and is justified, everything that is coded and moves in 'the flood of possible transformations' (1992: 279). It is the extreme limit of the subject, his final signature, his immaterial uniqueness. Just a Letter: to express the originary 'breath' of spirit, its wandering. A vain breath—but which moves upon the chaos.

BIBLIOGRAPHY

Aristotle. 2011. *Nicomachean Ethics*. Trans. R.C. Bartlett and S.D. Collins. Chicago: The University of Chicago Press.

Blanchot, Maurice. 1993. *The Infinite Conversation*. Trans. S. Hanson. Minneapolis and London: University of Minnesota Press.

---

[51] The reader will recognize the famous line from Vladimir Jankélévitch's *L'Irréversible et la nostalgie*: 'Whoever has been can never again not have been: from now on this mysterious and profoundly obscure fact of having lived is her viaticum for eternity' (1992: 339).

[52] Commenting on Chap. VI of the *Phenomenology*, Kojève characterizes the relationships within the Family in analogous terms: '[...] Society (the State) is concerned with the *Tun*, with the *action* of the individual, while the family attributes a value to his *Sein*, to his *being*, pure and simple, that is, to this nothingness and to his death. [...] Addressing the inactive being (*Sein*) of the brother, she [the sister] expects nothing from him; this is why the brother's death changes nothing for her' (1992: 100–101).

In a chapter entitled 'What Is, Is,' Patrick Guyomard returns to this identification by Lacan of the uniqueness of the brother (which is that of Antigone herself) and the symbolic cut (represented by the Signifier): 'The dead brother's uniqueness becomes the *pure* [...] relationship of Antigone with that which makes her a speaking subject; she identifies with the cut of language' (1992: 43). But in Sophocles' system, Guyomard stresses, 'this uniqueness includes incest' (1992: 44). Antigone's autonomy thus supposes a tragic trap and the shift from a deliberate claim to a deathly incestuous desire. Lacan does not denounce this confusion of the law (which is to say, of castration and language) with incest.

Borges, Jorge Luis. 1998. The Secret Miracle. In *Collected Fictions*, trans. A. Hurley, 82–85. London: Penguin.

Derrida, Jacques. 1986. *Glas*. Trans. J.P. Leavy and R. Rand. Lincoln: University of Nebraska Press.

Freud, Sigmund. 1895/1950. Project for a New Scientific Psychology. In *The Standard Edition* 1, 281–397. London: Hogarth Press.

Freud, Sigmund. 1915/1957. Instincts and Their Vicissitudes. Trans. J. Strachey. In *Standard Edition* 14, 117–140. London: Hogarth Press.

Freud, Sigmund. 1920/1961. *Beyond the Pleasure Principle*. Trans. J. Strachey. New York: WW Norton.

Freud, Sigmund. 1925/1961. Negation. Trans. J. Strachey. In *Standard Edition* 19, 235–239. London: Hogarth Press.

Freud, Sigmund. 1930/1961. *Civilization and Its Discontents*. Trans. J. Riviere. London: Hogarth Press.

Freud, Sigmund. 1930/2000. *Le Malaise dans la culture*. Trans. J. André. Paris: Presses Universitaires de France.

Hegel, G.W.F. 2018. *The Phenomenology of Spirit*. Trans. M. Inwood. Oxford: Oxford University Press.

Kant, Emmanuel. 1997. *The Critique eject because it torments him yet proves to b of Practical Reason*. Trans. M.J. Gregor. Cambridge: Cambridge University Press.

Kojève, Alexandre. 1973. The Idea of Death in the Philosophy of Hegel: (Complete Text of the Last Two Lectures of the Academic Year 1933–34). Trans. J.J. Carpino. *Interpretation* 3/2,3, 114–156.

———. 1997. *Introduction à la lecture de Hegel: Leçons sur la* Phénoménologie de l'Esprit. Ed. R. Queneau. Paris: Gallimard.

Kristeva, Julia. 1987. *Black Sun: Depression and Melancholy*. Trans. L.S. Roudiez. New York: Columbia University Press.

Lacan, Jacques. 1986. *Le Séminaire de Jacques Lacan: Livre Vii: L'éthique De La Psychanalyse 1959–1960*. Ed. J-A. Miller. Paris: Seuil.

———. 1992. *The Seminar: Book VII: The Ethics of Psychoanalysis 1959–1960*. Ed. J-A. Miller and trans. D. Porter. New York: WW Norton.

———. 2001. *Écrits: A Selection*. Trans. A. Sheridan. London: Routledge.

Laplanche, J., and J.B. Pontalis. 1973. *The Language of Psycho-Analysis*. Trans. D. Nicholson-Smith. London: The Hogarth Press.

Nietzsche, Frederick. 1999. *The Birth of Tragedy and Other Writings*. Trans. R. Speirs. Cambridge: Cambridge University Press.

Steiner, George. 1996. *Antigones: How the Antigone Legend Has Endured in Western Literature, Art, and Thought*. Yale: Yale University Press.

CHAPTER 7

The Fluidity of Being: *The Kabbalah*

Abstract This chapter explores new ways to respond to the quest for the absolute, a quest anchored in the heart of man, and which in the West so often takes on the aspect of death. Drawing on the Hebraic tradition, and in particular the Kabbalah, we try to work out a different mode of the absolute—one that is not enclosed in the *sphere* of perfection, but that, on the contrary, opens onto becoming and the indeterminate. This metaphysics of the unfinished, represented by the *straight line*, can then align with the very movement of life.

Keywords Circle • Straight line • Metaphysics • Disorder • Becoming

The thought of unhappiness, as it seems at present, is the product less of the languor of despair than of the excess of revolt. Contra the insipidity of fixed answers, it brings to incandescence the demand for a life that is larger and freer, befitting the new man. A man who has expanded to the dimensions of the universe, disturbed by ceaseless atoms, and who 'prefers the uneven meter.'[1] Greedy for the infinitely porous, devoted to the unstable, he espouses the multiple, in order to be authentically. He gives himself to death as one goes toward space, as one breathes, in the name of a bottomless expectation, which classical metaphysics has not been able to meet.

---

[1] The reader will recognize Verlaine's 'L'art poétique.'

© The Author(s) 2020
B. Rojtman, *The Fascination with Death in Contemporary French Thought*, https://doi.org/10.1007/978-3-030-47322-8_7

Could this mad aspiration, at the foundation of our humanity, find its immediate horizon at the beating heart of all life? Is there the chance to touch the infinite, without laying waste the present? To reinvent the absolute—a modality of being that would expand, sunder itself, in accord with our changeable nature? An absolute without frontiers, that would not have death as its sole guarantor and sole beginning. In the image of non-Euclidian geometry, a 'non-Platonic' metaphysics that would be centrifugal, dispersed, and whose perfection, moving and apertured, would offer consciousness a path on the earth. Is there a construction of plenitude that would deconstruct a priori and would open onto uncertainty? One which would be capable of representing the strange inside its own configuration, undoing the alternative of within and without, overcoming the perfect with an excess without end? In a word, can one imagine a post-modern metaphysics, pure of any immobility, broken free of the enchantment of the circle? A Law without rule, confusing its bearings, mixing its signals, that would shake up Time with an uncontrollable tremor?

For death would then no longer be the answer, no longer shine in the firmament of our metamorphoses. Death that is the other side, the sole exit, the only trek toward the immense. This metaphysics of the unfinished, that would have us think the unheard of, the *beyond* in the sense of surplus and ever renewed questioning, we propose to go in search of it, at the end of long journey, in the Hebraic sources of the occidental Bible, in the mystical Jewish source—which came in contact with occidental metaphysics, as we well know, by way of undergrounds streams, criss-cross paths and strange deformations.[2]

For this tradition, turned toward the future, has as its primary trait that it engraves the absolute with the very hallmark of the human, unsure, and always redefined, with the hallmark of a life-without-end that carries with it the unthought and becoming. To the Hebraic sensibility, the indefinite and spectacular which nothingness might promise can be more surely found at the surging center of the possible, at the tumultuous heart of our life, life which is in itself—and to itself—the elsewhere and astonishment, at the tumultuous heart where the wild adventure of existing unfolds.

---

[2]For an analysis of the underground streams which have led from Hebraic thought to contemporary philosophy, I would refer you to Marlène Zarader's courageous and painstaking book *The Unthought Debt: Heidegger and the Hebraic Heritage*: 'My hypothesis is that, beyond just theology, it is the history and thought of the west, taken as a whole, that carries this heritage, if quietly' (2006: 152).

If it does basically subscribe to the thesis of human exceptionalism, rabbinic commentary does not, however, conceive of man's existence as a foreign grain, a non-native seed in an indifferent universe. If Adam is only created on the sixth day, it is because his kingdom is first being readied *on earth*: he must be born to a world that awaits him. His relationship with the real will not be one of distrust but of accommodation, a concordance, in harmony with God's Work.

In the eyes of the monotheism of Israel, the clay is a welcome, the hidden side of a still unripened radiance: it is there that the Jewish man seeks his absolute, without renunciation, without abstraction, without monastic withdrawal. The Hebraic wager is to trust oneself to the impurity of the crystal, to the grain of sand, to everything that constitutes the erosion, the pain of living, and the unknown in every day. Judaic holiness takes the Creation into account, rather than constructing itself in opposition to it; the Idea in itself is no longer exterior, immaculate; on the contrary, it flows out into the concrete, and turns away from plenitude, toward the incomplete.

The mysterious character of this correlation, at the confluence of the human and the mineral, is underlined by the Hasidic tradition. Our existential milieu is created by the inscription of light in the inanimate: an incomprehension, an algorithm that poses, in its way, the question of the limit. No longer between life and death, but between subject and substance—entities incommensurable one with the other, at once permeable to one another and out of phase. At the seam of these two realms, the 'divine decree'—from the Hebrew work *'hok*, *'huka*, which means 'chisel mark' 'engraved inscription'—manifests the irrational of the conjunction and traces in the sands the mark of a meaning to be revealed.[3]

Contrary to the Kojévian approach,[4] it is therefore at the heart of the multiple, in a continual interaction, that, in the Jewish conception, man

---

[3] Cf. Alter (1872/2000), Parashat Para: 'The meaning of the word "decree" refers to the form which the Eternal wanted to impress on matter [...] and which animates it from within. [...] Therefore, the commandments relating to the natural world seem arbitrary [irrational] to us, [...] – while the truths of a uniquely spiritual order are accessible to reason.'

[4] Kojève, you will remember, referred Hegelian anthropology back to a *Judeo-Christian* origin, which is to say, according to him, a dualist tradition: 'Nature is a "sin" in Man and for Man: He can and must *oppose* himself to it and *negate* it in himself' (Kojève 1973: 120, in italics in the text). It is not our intention to subscribe to this somewhat over-rapid conflation or to reduce the complexity of Christian theology. We want only, in response to Kojévian radicalism, to draw out the principles of one of the currents of the Hebraic heritage.

bears witness to his uniqueness as human. The universe is his place, secretly in accord with his most immaterial aspirations. The Midrash paints the Creator consulting the Torah before setting to work,[5] careful from the start to provide these furtive responsorials, these hidden correspondences that will allow the Spirit to unfurl itself over the earth. The world, like man, changes and becomes; its numberless branches sway across time.

To ensure its dignity, it will therefore no longer be necessary for consciousness to differentiate itself from Nature, to understand itself by means of opposition. Man belongs to the world, no longer as an animal, but in fact by virtue of his liberty, as inalienable transcendence. The fragmentation, the freeing from restraint, that attest his difference, will no longer find their sustenance in the abyss: it is the universe in itself that already palpitates with a syncopal and labored breath. Its porous tissue, traversed with flashes of light, spreads out in intangible threads, in a spider's web of possibles. Thus, man no longer awaits death to undo his moorings: his presence in the real is already dispersion, infinitude. It is in the world that he manages to escape, by an effort of processing, of filtering, of innovating, which dissolves the apparent fixity of the elements, and gives them back the shimmer of indeterminacy.

In this negotiation, the law of Moses plays the role of an instruction manual: a means of refining the ponderous, of giving clay back its subtlety. This is the sense of religious practice: to prefer the *corps à corps* with the immediate, to take the cosmos into the march of History. In a certain respect, the Jew, therefore, plays the slave against the master: like the former, he becomes a man by his work on the sensible world and the suspending of his own *jouissance*; like him, he subjects the 'raw' given (Kojève 1997: 28) to a civilizing action, breaking at the same time his own dependence on conditionings, gaining access through this task to his liberty. But the goal of this 'progressive transformation of the World' (Kojève 1997: 28), of the accent placed on 'change' and 'autonomy' (1997: 27), is not to break the bond that ties the person to the universe. The 'work' of the Law aims, on the contrary, to reveal, under the opacity of the crust, under the appearance of hardened lava, Nature's spiritual concordance, its profound ontological plasticity, its vocation to indeterminacy.

This transaction with the concrete will take all of History's time. Once it turns away from the caesura and from death, to open itself, on the

---

[5] Cf. *Bereshith Rabba* 1:1: 'The Holy One, Blessed Be He, gazed into the Torah and created the world.'

contrary, to that which is, this maturation implies a dependence, a repercussion of matter on spirit: which is to say a threat of defilement, a calling
into a question of the absolute. To what extent can Jewish metaphysics
admit this corruption and take into account the 'failing' of the world, in
the sense of chance and errancy? Between earth and heaven, the rabbinic
decisors are torn, each one seeking, according to his own religious sensibility, the right proportion, the golden ratio of a difficult combinatorial
problem; inclining rather, depending on the case, toward a rigor in the
ancient style, or more audaciously committed to groping in obscurity.
How is one to live here below when one believes in heaven? How is one
to construct eternity from a base of daily error? The interweaving of the
plural and the one, of the contingent and the necessary, brings ambiguity
into the very detail of observances and behaviors. Walking straight into the
whirlwind of life, the duty of faith falters in the face of the unforeseeable.
How is one to assume these failures, these missteps, these slippages, when
it is a question of reaching truth? What meaning is one to give to the
'more or less,' if the soul grates against the needs of life, if pure accident,
understood as escaping restraint and as freedom, clashes with the persis-
tent dream of the imperishable?

This philosophical risk reaches one of its highpoints in the example of
the declaration of the new month. The Hebraic calendar, as is well known,
is a mixed calendar, combining in one model the staggered cycles of moon
and sun. But this double periodization is not really shared out equally: in
Jewish historic and symbolic consciousness, the counting of lunar months
far prevails over that of years and seasons. Israel's relationship with tem-
porality, its understanding of the stars, its symbolic identity,[6] does not
pertain centrally to the sun, but to the moon: troubled, intermittent,
indeterminable. Doesn't the first commandment given in the Bible require
that one sanctify the new month as soon as the crescent shows (Exodus
12:1–2)? But in the vault of the constellations, the lunar path is distinguished by its irregularity; the course of the months never falls just right,
but changes from lunar month to lunar month, and is felt by the tradition
as a capricious rhythm, as an irruption of the sporadic into solar
imperturbability:

---

[6] Cf. Epstein (1905/2006: 426, § 2). 'The children of Israel, who base their calendar on
the movement of the moon, have been compared to the moon.'

> Rabbi Yo'hanan teaches: "He made the moon to mark the time, the sun knows the end of its path" (Ps. 104, 19): only the sun knows the end of its path; the moon, for its part, knows nothing of it. (*Babylonian Talmud, Rosh Hashana*, 25 a)

In this balletic dance of the stars, which follow and miss each other along the axis of time, the dialectic re-emerges, crystal and smoke. The sun represents the certain cycle, the return of the star at fixed intervals, the immobile brilliance of circularities. The moon, on the other hand, marks the profusion of possibles, a flow of inconstancy in the stellar eurythmia.

In order to fix the date of Jewish festivals, the Talmud must therefore reconcile the cadences, bring incompatibles together, at the intersection of the eternal and the living. It appears then that the legislator, far from seeking to reduce the discordances, rather privileges, as if by caprice, the random of the lunar rhythm: abandoning the astronomical certainties that are theirs, the Court of Sages, in order to decide on the new month, trusts the observation of eye-witnesses, despite all that this choice supposes of hypothetical and hazardous. As if there were no other response to the *différance* but difference itself, and that human weakness alone could ally, in the cosmos of exactitudes, the ambivalence of the visible with the happenstances of the 'more or less.'

This position of ambiguity, that opts for the unregulated, and integrates variation into its concept of the absolute, leads the religious sensibility to an impasse. It was not without pain, says the Talmud (*Babylonian Talmud, Rosh Hashana*, 25 a), that Rabbi Yehoshua, still skeptical before the deposition of one of the witnesses, opposed Rabban Gamaliel—then president of the tribunal—who chose to ratify it. At this moment of intense spiritual crisis, the dissenter is called on to give way and to thereby disavow his own evaluations. In order to display his obedience, he must go to the house of his superior in travel attire, on the very day on which, according to his calculations, Kippur should fall. In this poignant scene, in which Rabbi Yehoshua arrives before the president of the Sanhedrin 'with his stick and his money,' is acted out the drama inherent in the religious consciousness: if the Day of Atonement gives absolution just by its happening, can it be moved, even by only a day? Is its ontological power maintained, its metaphysical and astral justness, when it is thus exposed to the margin of error, to the sensorial blurriness of the human? Who knows what theological catastrophe lies in wait under this profanation, what collapse behind these dilatory reasonings, these effects of ignorance and miscalculation.

The moderns have preferred to see, in this debate, a pure conflict of authority. The real discord is elsewhere. Philosophical, spiritual, it pushes us to reconsider the sidereal absolute, its chronological purposiveness, the sacramental justice of a day that '*in itself* offers expiation' (cf. *Babylonian Talmud, Yoma* 85 b and Maimonides, *Mishneh Torah, Hilkhot Tshuva*: Chap. I, 3). How far can the truth of Time thus bear to be stretched? How far can it—or perhaps *should it*—deny itself, to cast anchor beyond, in some harmony of transgression? Can one envisage a deconstruction of the exact, which alone would ensure the concordance of cycles, at the end of all the deviations? In the name of what asymmetrical perfection—free-flowing, laid open, that would embrace in its meanders the inconsistencies of life? In the name of what piecemeal plenitude, woven of torn threads, and that would fill itself in only with lack and splices?

Rabbi Yehoshua returns home desolate—from this hurt to the soul that will not ease. Rabbi Akiva, his student, visits him and finds him prostrate in the darkest of sorrows. At this moment, the disciple reminds the master of a forgotten teaching that offers him the key to the system: there is an eternity without horizon, a repetition of stars, that can be healed only by the ephemeral. There is a truth forged of errors which, going back to the source of meaning, grounds there a supreme concomitance—that of the differential:

Akiva continued: 'Master, allow me to remind you here of one of your own teachings: [...] "These are the feasts of the Eternal, holy convocations, which *you*[7] will celebrate in their seasons" (*Leviticus* 23:4). [...] It is *you* who will fix the date of these feasts—*you, even though you make a mistake*, even though you (deliberately) falsify the dating, even if someone has deceived you.' Rabbi Yehoshua then responded in these terms: 'Akiva, you have consoled me, you have consoled me.' (*Babylonian Talmud, Rosh Hashana* 25 a, our italics)

The consolation comes from this prescience, that there exists a solemnity in the perhaps, that one should accept the contingent. The divine is sprinkled with false steps, vacillations and accidents. That is its kingdom on earth. Jewish metaphysics has set itself the task of embracing the froth of the days: a 'broken leaf of ivy [...] a step fading in the night' (Blanchot

---

[7] The formula is repeated three times in one chapter, which deals with the calendar of feasts. Three times, the text repeats the pronoun *otam* [you will celebrate *them*]. But this word can also be read *atem*, 'you': it is *you* who will celebrate them.

1993: 34). All that trembles and falls, the surprise of the possible like the wanderings of thought. It is why the 'embolismic' adjustment of the lunar calendar to the solar rhythm,[8] the accommodation of the erratic to the regular, will rely, for the Talmud, on purely circumstantial indicators: the state of the roads or of the bread ovens, damaged by the winter rains, the maturation of the barley in the fields, the progress of pilgrims going to Jerusalem (cf. *Babylonian Talmud, Sanhedrin*, 11a et 11b). An insignificant and abundant everyday—a *there is* without horror—which, in the Jewish idea, can reach the heavens without changing the heavens' light. Rather, it inflects it, extends it with a flash of disorder, with an uneven flow, which swerves the immutable firmaments toward the moving infinite.

What happens to us in the mayhem of hours, what surprises us at the turn of the road, is part of a supreme Precision. The event under way, its chiaroscuro, its unknown, are exact expressions of the divine plan: at once anarchy of circumstances and programmed meticulousness. Between 'determination' (*mikra*) and 'chance' (*mikré*), the terms, the sounds and syllables, are interchangeable throughout the Bible (cf. Hacohen 1922/1972: §3 p. 164),[9] between 'feast' and 'fortuitousness,' between 'incident' and 'prophesy,' as if to indicate an intrinsic proximity, an ontological affinity at the base of Jewish experience. The originality of commentary is to show the correlation of the levels, which overlap without merging. If Providence wears the face of the fortuitous, it is because it gives a chance to the unforeseeable and because it bends the Project to the zigzags of the human:

> Speak unto the children of Israel, and say unto them: the feasts of the Eternal which *you* celebrate as holy convocations, even these are *My* feasts. (*Leviticus* 23:2). Whether they are celebrated in their seasons *or whether they are not*, I recognize them as *My feasts.* (*Babylonian Talmud, Rosh Hashanah*, 25 a, our italics)

The Eternal takes upon Himself the drift of time. The absolute is not annulled as such; it is recomposed, entrusts itself to precariousness, to the point of welcoming confusion, of welcoming the dissonance that floats

---

[8] The 'embolismic' adjustment orders that one intercalate, at irregular intervals, a thirteenth lunar month into the sidereal year, in order to maintain the correspondence between the phases of the moon and the rhythm of the seasons.

[9] Cf. Hacohen (1922/1972), *Vayikra, Emor.* § 3, D.h. '*Moadei Hashem asher tikrcu otam,*' p. 164.

above our lives. The principle of a certitude without assurance, of an erod-ing totality, regulates by its contradictory logic the becoming of the worlds. Standing opposite to the calculable, metahistorical, pulsations that regulate the universal, there is a different rhythm, more jolting, harsher and nourished on the arbitrary, through which arises the unthought.[10]

The wager of the Jewish faith has been to integrate this philosophy of the ambiguous—and all of the contingency and incertitude that it carries with it—into metaphysics itself. The vicissitudes of life, which is to say, its shocks, its drifts, its misunderstandings, are an integral part of spiritual objectivity and contribute to defining it. Human experience is played out inside of plenitude; it brings fragmentation and inexactitude to the heart of the truth, imposes a gap in the idea of the whole. As if it were a question of promoting a form of fulfillment that was hitherto unseen, and paradoxi-cal. An idea of perfection that stays open, resolutely the antithesis of the immobile, and conceived from the start as indeterminate and changing. A totality still moist, still riven and flowing, maintaining its status of ideality, but in lack; an irregularity that pours into the One—but in order to per-vert it, to deform it, to sublate it from within, working it through with a fertile excess. The circle is broken, torn by some ray of Light, some light-ning flash that streaks it through with the unknown. The Hebraic absolute is without determination, open to a range of transformations, resonating with approximations and dreams.

This pattern of intersection, which posits the synergy of incompatible forces, finds its source in mystical cosmogony. For the Lurianic Kabbalah would have it that two processes of emanation are initiated in the begin-ning, and dovetail and intertwine: the first, that represented by the sphere, generates the natural universe; the other, which refers more generally to the life of the spirit, is represented by an infinite straight line. The two orders cross, marry their inverse roles, which Jewish monotheism has as its task to bring together. The meeting, nonetheless, is mysterious: it never falls out *just right*. Its rough exactitude, always postponed, is placed, in the commentary, under the ever-receding aegis of the number Pi,[11] in which is concentrated the strange complexity of life. Behind this equilibrium always in the making, and never finally achieved, cross-hatched with circles and

---

[10] Cf. *Babylonian Talmud, Sanhedrin*, 97 a: 'Three things happen to us unexpectedly [in "distraction"]: the Messiah, the find, and the scorpion's sting.' See also on this theme Rojtman (1991).

[11] Cf. Askénazi (1987).

lines, an insistent hierarchy emerges, which gives preference to the straight line: which is to say, to the surge without recoil, to the obstinacy of the new, to the inexhaustible breath of the ongoing.

Genesis describes to us first, on the immediately visible surface, a world strangely close to the Greek Logos. The same completeness, it seems, the same closure, the same periodicity. Day after day, each element takes its place in the vast diagram of Creation that grounds determinations and overcomes Chaos. *Elohim*, the name by which the Almighty manifests Himself, is associated in the exegesis with this form of the absolute that regulates the rhythms and contours in Nature. It creates in separating, it assigns systems and functions. The God of the beginning is a God of the limit,[12] who impresses onto measurelessness measurable movements.

Yet this harmony of the first days represents only an inferior mode of revelation—a prelude, a start. For the Judaic sensibility, this gyration of the stars, this string of causes and effects,[13] expresses rather opacity, the 'fall' and the unfulfillment of the earth: a rationality inspired with lack, deficient in its very perfection.

For, according to the Lurianic cosmogony, the image of the sphere is born with the *tzimtzum* ('contraction' or 'withdrawal'). The Light from before all worlds is still undifferentiated, overabundant and continuous, hermetic by dint of plenitude, saturated with transparency. 'Diminution' is required in order to carve out, in this excess, an area of nothingness, a gaping and desolate crater, that is uncovered at low tide. For it is at the heart of this empty space, of this darkness hollowed out in the Infinite, that the universe will be located and that it can be brought into being: the gleam left as pledge by the Withdrawal adapts itself to the curve of life; it curves itself and sketches, in the form of a number of orbs, the contours of a Cosmos to come. Ten concentric emanations thus represent, in the firmament of the Kabbalah, the primitive pattern of Creation:

> The [first] *sfirot* [emanations], which draw more directly from the Light left in traces [...] in the primordial Void, are part [as *it* is] of the order of the circle. (Beuman 1937/1977: 114)[14]

---

[12] *El Shaddaï*: 'He who has put bounds on his world.' Cf. the teaching of Reish Lakish: *Babylonian Talmud, Haguiga*, 12 a.

[13] 'All beings are derived one from another, intertwined in each other according to cause and effect, in the universal logic of the sphere' (Haver: 23).

[14] The few elements of Kabbalah presented here are simplified in the extreme. The particular (complex) point of origin of the first *sfirot* has been the object of various interpretations.

Therefore, everything that comes to being will feel the effects of this initial hollowing, of this necessary removal which forms the dark—and as if germinal—side of Creation. An ontology marked by *tzimtzum*, imprinted with this breach from the start, by this matrix convexity that reduces its scope. The sphere in its unity, in its very closure, thus appears here as incomplete: it has its origin in loss, in keeping with loss's logic, one of night and austerity. Everything that is generated from this primary and void sphere will keep, for the Kabbalah, some taste of lack, a distancing and something like a diminishing of the Idea.

It is thus not by chance that this eurythmia, weak from the outset because of its exactitude and its periodicity, only manages to express itself in the impassivity of the workings and the chain of reasons. Marked with the double seal of precision and the impersonal, the ten circular '*sfirot*' distribute the vital Breath according to a law of numbers, imperturbably following the classes and the levels of being—without regard for the individual, his effort or even his existence:

> The general conduct of the universe establishes a natural order, insensible to the movements of consciousness. Energy flows there evenly, dispensing life to all created beings. This form of governance relates to the circle, in the sense that the sphere marks equidistance from all points, without distinction of direction—right or left, up or down. In the same way, its regime is undifferentiated, and tends neither toward Rigor nor toward Goodness. The Eternal gives life uniformly to all his creatures, in accordance with their very essence, each one according to what it *is*. (Haver: 22, our italics)[15]

This egalitarianism heralds, in some ways, Greek eternity. Without sharp angles, any break, or any beginning, the sphere's is an unbreathable justice. But the Kabbalah sees, in this too-well-oiled mechanism, only a framework, an encirclement to be broken. Accident must prevail: alteration, asymmetry, all that re-activates and goes forth.

It is then that a new ray of Light penetrates space, with its descending beam. A long brilliant flash that soars across the Void, that crosses in order to add something, to correct absence. Eager to flow out, fated to surplus, it is the Idea in its impulse, always more, always further, toward the invisible and receding point of its revelation. The straight line is without

---

Rav Beuman, who belongs to the Hasidic ('habad) tradition, himself indicates in a note the limits to his own point of view. I use it here, nonetheless, for the sake of its clarity.

[15] This author is associated with the Lithuanian school of Vilna Gaon.

concept, without fixity, without completeness. A sparkling and liquid entity, a pulsating image of the eternal, it pertains to a kind of infinite that is stronger than the totality, unfurling itself without ever halting, free of all attachment, and cleaving through the future:

> The dimension of the Straight Line is what is essential in the universe; it prevails over the Circles, which are subordinate to it. The Straight Line, which is to say, the liberty of life, the absolute liberty poured out by the source of being, the liberty attached to the divine principle [...] it is everything! (Kook 1888/1985: 24)[16]

An innovatory figure because unrestrained, the vertical in its impulsion pierces the stellar absolute. In its radiant outpouring, it is transgressive and 'cuts a path beyond all the laws that stand in the way' (Kook 1888/1985: 25). In the style of Blanchot, it punctures the spherical space toward a 'beyond [...] achieved knowledge' (Blanchot 1993: 208), crossing through the rings all the better to escape them; it exceeds, it compensates for the inexorable, is subversively traced out in the heart of what it revives: taking on its task, drilling through perfection, it shoots beyond, transcending the 'wholeness' which seemed forever condemned to paralysis:

> At the heart of the Circles themselves, of the rigid regulations of the universe, of these iron laws that never change, whether applying to nations or to individuals [...]; at the heart of these forces, the Straight Line intervenes and acts, subjects them to its influence. (Kook 1888/1985: 25)

The sparkle of this line does not fill anything in, cannot seal anything off. Limited to this pure ray of energy, to this narrow beam, without extension or area, it has no identity but the dynamic. Going straight on its path, drawn on by the future, relentless and sustained. When the arches of the world become too stiff, too refractory to movement, too curled up on themselves and on their immobile curvature, the line hits them full on, with its shining stream breaks the log jam, everything that hinders and checks its flow. The Kabbalah gives the name *Tohu*[17] to this threat of

---

[16] For this fundamental opposition between the sphere and the straight line, see Askénazi (1973, esp. pp. 92–93).

[17] The reader will recognize the second verse of *Genesis*: 'Now the earth was only desert [*Tohu*] and chaos.' Again it was Rav Beuman who, in a remarkable feat of synthesis, assimilated the '*sfirot*' of circularity with the superior but untenable world of *Tohu*.

collision, this discordance of the circle and the straight line, this competition between two forms of absolute—which in the end causes the Vessels to break.[18]

The torrent of Light has forced its way into the autarchy of each world, its self-containment and its unity. The breaking of the vessels is a little death, the end of a homogenous and compact dream. But it opens onto the diverse, the unforeseeable implied in the sowing of seeds: chaos can only be overcome by the multiple.[19] To the reign of disorder (*Tohu*) succeeds that of *Tikun* (or 'repair'); it brings with it the dissemination, a scattering of grain, like a subtle pollen.

The ray of Light is then configured in ten new emanations: these are the *sfirot* of the Straight line, assigned to the atomization of possibles and the establishment of a relationship between them. The Light that comes back is no longer that burnished, even luster of equanimity. Rather, it differentiates, forms branches, adapts itself to the variations in the given; the real has become unnumberable. From now on, the ray that pours out admits interactions, an osmosis between beings; it adapts to the slippage of hierarchies. In this second, linear phase of the emanation, in this superior and regenerational phase, which acquiesces to the Creation and wants to secure it, the energy divides in order to better radiate: split into three vertical axes, it now spreads out along parallel vectors, in accord with life's shimmering relations, its translatory movements and its degrees. Diving into the ideal ether, torn from the orbit of the Whole, it gives itself by diffraction to the rainbow of postures: progressions, regressions, modifications of points of view—a vast respiration of beings and things, that displaces truths and upsets accepted markers. Each entity defines itself in the end by its tending toward the more-than-itself, differing from itself across the ages, in the rhythm of infinitesimal oscillations:

> The second modality is that of the Straight Line [...] All creatures are subject, under its influence, to a differential regime, which concerns each individual in the detail of his being, and deflects into various levels, according to Rigor or Mercy, good or evil, the rise or the fall. (Haver: 23)

[18] This reading refers, though in a slightly modified form, to the classical theory of the 'breaking of the vessels,' which in the Kabbalah grounds the relationship between the light and its receptacles: according to this dialectic, it is the point without extension, solipsistic, the autonomy proper to the receptacle, when it withdraws into its perfection and its singularity, that symbolically prevents the absorption of the light.

[19] Cf. the preceding note.

It is no surprise, at the end of the day, that this 'variable-geometry' metaphysics also marks, by its very fluidity, by its a-priori indetermination, Man's entrance on the scene, and his responsibility in the cosmological evolution.[20] For the Kabbalah—already for the Midrash—the world seems to have been created only on condition, in the name of this second moment, this modulation in essence, which ensures the transition toward the existential. A passage from the undifferentiated to the individual, from the impersonal to the person, from eternity to History: in keeping with the occidental perception, Jewish tradition confers an anthropological meaning on the becoming of the universe, on its turbulence and its sway-ing. This is why the three axes of Light trace, symbolically, the contours of the human silhouette: with his extended limbs, immemorial and straight, primordial Man[21] links the planes of revelation one to the other. Which is to say that the cosmic stream of energy adapts to the curve of human des-tinies, that it arranges itself by their fluctuations, sensible to the modifica-tions of this essentially incomplete creature, who 'knows no respite,' who, 'on the contrary, moves relentlessly and strives to attain his own perfec-tion' (Loew ben Bezalel 1589/1971, 2:8).

By its back and forth, by the limitlessness of its extension, the modality of the straight line thus represents, and carries, the passion of the con-sciousness, the asymptotic tension of a surge that trembles unceasingly toward tomorrow, and is increased even in its moments of decline. The homology of the spiritual and the cosmic vibrations underlines the corre-lation of these linear movements progressing forward to the same goal: it is 'as a function of human ethics' that 'the condition of creatures varies, [that] it rises or falls, [that] it absorbs more or less Light' (Haver: 23). Moral consciousness here plays the role of ferment, of dialectical drive in the universal revolution, that makes glow, 'in the seeming shadows of determinism, the emerging flash of liberty' (Kook 1888/1985: 25).[22]

With the coming of Adam, on the sixth day, it is therefore a new ratio-nale that unfolds, a *rectitude*[23] now *en route*, in the name of a seed sowing

---

[20] Cf. Askénazi (1973: 92). 'Simultaneously, therefore, [...] the "divine project" has two dimensions [...]: the straight line that becomes the form of the human face, and the sphere that becomes the form of the impersonal world.'

[21] 'Primordial man' or *Adam Kadmon* represents in the Lurianic Kabbalah the first level of emanation of being. The closest to the origin, it contains within it, virtually, all the worlds to come.

[22] The liberty in question here is that of moral will.

[23] In Hebrew the root *YoSHeR* means at once 'straight' and 'rectitude.'

that will have no end. If the linear structure is thus privileged, it is because it alone is aimed at 'the founding principle of Creation' (Kook 1888/1985: 24), the true abode of man: a world according to the Idea, as if animated by so much endless rising and falling, perpetually becoming, drawing closer to itself, and ever missing itself.

For the light of the Straight Line, its free-flowing profusion, cannot, as such, pervade life nor reveal the full extent of its splendor. Its role is to make the dull resonate, to set the shadows aflame, in the rhythm of its bursting forth: but as soon as it realizes itself, as soon as it takes a particular form in order to appear, it reduces itself. Diminished and distorted by this very crystallization, losing in this determination its aerial intensity, its flow of essentiality:

> The absolute Idea,[24] in manifesting itself, empties itself of its authenticity. [...] If it sows, in its appearing, the seeds of good and rectitude, if the drops of justice then flow from the divine source, one must nevertheless suppose that there subsists, in each creature, in each form in which the Idea is *concretized*, signs of negativity and of Breakage. (Sterlitz 1966: 146, our italics)[25]

For every configuration is already loss, every effective presence a decrease of being, the breakdown of a radiant but misdirected potentiality. In taking form, in stopping, the protean energy is degraded, to the degree that it reveals itself. The actual restrains, adulterates, constricts. While Light crosses bars[26] and frontiers, while the immense is in us at our gates, more than us at every instant, scything down in order to bring together, harvest after harvest, flinging out its negation like so many seeds. The beam flies ahead and gives of itself, makes itself reality, gives itself existence. But by its vivifying flow, each emergence, each generated circumstance, instantly is broken. The straight line is this foray toward the real

[24] This citation is taken from a commentary by Rav Sterlitz (1966), which is of a more ethical character than Kabbalistic. The key terms, therefore, shift in comparison with the terminology adopted by Rav Kook in *Orot Hakodesh* (1888/1985) and used in our chapter. Nonetheless, both the 'absolute Idea' which is in question here and the 'Return' which comes up a little later on (cf. *infra*, note 27) correspond with what Rav Kook understood by 'the Straight Line.'

[25] The term 'Breakage' refers to the breaking of the vessels which we mentioned earlier: this process is considered continuous, repeated at all levels of the history of Creation, like most of the processes described by the Lurianic cosmogony.

[26] [Translator's note: Again the maritime image of leaving the bay which Tennyson uses in his famous poem.]

that at the same time denies itself, that renounces its own path, its vocation to nourish, to define existence—in a sort of 'radical negation' toward that which is higher than itself, in a sort of constitutive impatience that denies its own work, continually revived in a progress without end:

> The Return[27] is this aspiration to deliverance that [...] tends to free itself of all expression, of all specific form or configuration, for the benefit of new realizations, each time more crystalline and more pure, each time closer to the source [...] It proceeds from a perpetual dissatisfaction, inscribed in the very heart of the created. [...] A fruitful, vital dissatisfaction, that makes new lands, new dimensions emerge. [...] Thus the cosmos does not limit itself to a defined state; it evolves, on the contrary, and develops continually. (Sterlitz 1966: 147)

This process has as its horizon a transparency to come, ceaselessly lost and ceaselessly restored. It carries Creation into an ex-sistence beyond any circle, outside of the sclerotic identical. Outside of that which settles, calms or is completed. The spherical is aridity, failure and stagnation. The line, on the other hand, opens to the infinite, flying irrepressibly toward the being-more, fashioning the created, each time more just, each time closer to an ungraspable matrix. In an abundant and headstrong stream, the straight line carries in its headlong flow the alluvia of destroyed continents, of all that which rose to existence and has withered, of all that which is annihilated into metamorphosis.

This bottomless dialectic knows neither synthesis nor totalization. The spiral of approximations, emerging out of absence, sustained by negations, transcends eternity: it goes toward the greater, in the name of a truth always more eminent and unrepresentable, whose image dissipates as it draws near. There is no end to this lack, no summit or Hegelian plenitude. To live implies failure, a continuous amputation, wherein takes root redemptive becoming. There is, therefore, no longer thinkable any integrity, any process closed up in its 'already.' Nothing which exists can make any claim to serenity—fated rather to resumption, to pursuit, without anything being affirmed that must not be undone. The design of the straight line does not suppose completion: like death, it provides escape, it dissolves, disembodies; but from this empty space, from this pallid neutrality, it builds new presents; circle after circle, unfailingly negated, infinitely

---

[27] Cf. *supra*, note 24. The author defines the Return as 'consubstantial with the Idea.'

'sublated' by the drive of desire. It fissures the arc of the given, exceeding the possible, opening the breach of an Outside: experience of limit, on the edge of being, that each time skims and misses some messianic beyond, a virtual splendor, by definition unknowable. The condition of creature is thus at once death of being and expectation of being—a novel form of *between two*,[28] that resolves itself in movement; no longer only, in the style of Blanchot, in worklessness or retreat[29]—but by turmoil, an effervescence of light, an abandonment to the immense.

It is therefore an 'open' pattern of spirituality that the Kabbalah offers us, with its disorder, its renascent flow, its untamed floods. A metaphysics of fluidity that seems a presentiment, in the style of the moderns, of the necessary convergence of the void and of life, the secret efficacy of defeat, the alliance of the cut and the bursting forth. It affirms mutation in general: not only of energies or of matter but also of the values of truth, of the meaning of man and of his action. One can glimpse, under this tacking back and forth, that the refusal of satiety, and the breakage by which the Whole is opened and put into motion, can find routes other than that of devastation. That the opening and thirst, reduced to their deathly dimension by the West, orient Jewish morality toward a pre-Sartrean existentialism, of engagement and liberty—but tied to being. Ethics is one of the names of this breach in the One, of this wound, of this availability to the Strange—the priesthood of which Jewish mysticism entrusts to the human person.[30] Ethics conveys the image of a fracture, of a non-coincidence with oneself, which is what allows one to receive the influx, the repeated pulsation of a rejuvenation that ceaselessly vibrates and changes, as if between the banks of a river.

The creature allows itself to be permeated, it offers itself and receives: a surplus empties it, like an abyss of clarity. The miraculous fragility of the human, his inconsistency with himself, his presence as of a mist, are the given realities of life, even before turning to death. Rather, they represent a form of death, such a death as would accompany us, which clings to our

[28] Cf. Blanchot (1993: 209). 'man sees himself assigned - between being and nothingness, and out of the infinite of this between-two that is entertained as relation - the status of his new sovereignty: the sovereignty of a being without being in the becoming without end of a death impossible to die.'

[29] See, for example, Blanchot (1993: 210). 'advancing as though backward toward a point he only knows he will not reach in person.'

[30] One can see here, under the allegory, a 'sublating' of the ontological by the ethical, which the work of Levinas has familiarized us with.

side. But from which proceeds survival, at every instant porous and riven—a milk-white life, as if caressed by a gentle sun, always vulnerable, and enhanced by this very vulnerability. Man's role is to exist: to give himself to the ephemeral, in order to roll toward the infinite; to find support on the cloud, in order to contribute to the Return. Living is in itself a transparency, a trembling, called to destitution and to the crown.

It is by this acquiescence in the fallible, in the crumbling of what has been won, that consciousness participates in the absolute. It is this—worldly—labor in vain, this happiness in lack, that ensures the royalty of the moment, completes it and fulfills it, that builds it higher, unchangeable, closer to the enigma. The most internal rhythm unfolds thus into the greatest exteriority, the outside is an inside in search of itself. A mysterious disequilibrium perturbs the divisions and the limits, carries totality toward the unreason of the unstable.

Thus, the immutability of the sphere is only a moment of passage, only one of the faces of the Idea. The dissemination and the storm, human life, in its precariousness, remains the ultimate, ontological, standard of the surreal. Between reality and revelation, man is a bridge; he is himself the interval, the perishable and sovereign between-two. At least, always on the edge, entrusted with the destiny of Creation, at least he moves its confines little by little, patiently encroaching on the infinite, little by little gaining ground, conquering the beyond like an untilled field, by his piecemeal efforts that kindle the light.

BIBLIOGRAPHY

Alter, Yehuda Arieh Leib. 1872/2000. *Sefat Emet.* Merkaz Shapira: Yeshivat Or Etsion.

Askénazi, Léon. 1973. *La notion de sainteté dans la pensée du Rav Kook.* Twelfth Conference of French-Language Jewish Intellectuals: The Jews in a Desacralized Society, 31 October 1971. In *L'Autre dans la conscience juive, le sacré et le couple,* ed. J. Halpérin and G. Lévitte, 80–100. Paris: Presses Universitaires de France.

———. 1987. *Le 7 Adar (anniversaire de Moïse) et la fête de Pourim.* Lecture at Yaïr Center, Jerusalem.

Beuman, Shaul. 1937/1977. *Sefer Maphte'hei 'Hokhmat Haemet.* Jerusalem: No publisher.

Blanchot, Maurice. 1993. *The Infinite Conversation.* Trans. S. Hanson. Minneapolis and London: University of Minnesota Press.

Epstein, Ye'hiel Michel Halevi. 1905/2006. *Arukh Hashul'han, Ora'h 'Hayim.* No Publisher.

Hacohen, Zadok. 1922/1972. *Peri Zadik,* T. III, *Vayikra, Emor.* Jerusalem: Books Export Enterprises.

Kojève, Alexandre. 1973. The Idea of Death in the Philosophy of Hegel: (Complete Text of the Last Two Lectures of the Academic Year 1933–34). Trans. J.J. Carpino. *Interpretation* 3/2,3, 114–156.

———. 1997. *Introduction à la lecture de Hegel: Leçons sur la* Phénoménologie de l'Esprit. Ed. R. Queneau. Paris: Gallimard.

Kook, Avraham Yits'hak Hacohen. 1888/1985. *Orot Hakodesh* 2nd Part, Vol. 3 *Mussar Hakodesh.* Ed. D. Cohen. Jerusalem: Mossad Harav Kook.

Loew ben Bezalel, Yehuda. 1589/1971. *Derekh ha'Hayim.* Bnei Brak: Yahadut.

Rojtman, Betty. 1991. *Une grave distraction.* Paris: Balland.

Sterlitz, Shimeon. 1966. Hatsehuva leor histakluto shel rabenu. Appendix to Abraham Isaac Hacohen Kook, *Orot Hateshuva.* Merkaz Shapira: Yeshivat Or Etsion.

Zarader, Marlène. 2006. *The Unthought Debt: Heideger and the Hebraic Heritage.* Trans. B. Bergo. Stanford: Stanford University Press.

CHAPTER 8

Conclusion

Abstract At the end of this study, one senses that the desire for death is not in itself its own end, but rather the oblique expression of an aspiration toward difference, of a sidereal desire that nothing can fulfill. But life already offers us a breach into the infinite, through its very evanescence and its fluidity, which are the actual forms of transcendence.

Keywords Hunger to live • Icarus

The proximity of death sweeps away the dust, the banality and the boredom. It makes the difficult flame of our existing shine the more brightly. A bewitchment by death, in the name of more intense life, that gives up its secret only at the moment of dispossession. When we, vagabonds that we are, wandering a Beckettian universe, leave behind all our baggage, in order to limit ourselves to existence itself, hanging on the purely vital, on the illumination of the final moments. If the poet, in Bataille, exalts the horror of the last hour, it is in order to better enjoy a kernel of being, as if in a sun-struck stupor, that can be felt only in the savagery of the end. For 'when we enter the regions that wisdom tells us to avoid,' we attain to the tumult that is simply breathing. Rather than '*preserving life*,' '*we really live it*' (Bataille 2012: 64, in italics in the text) finally, profoundly, concentrated on this enigma. To that insatiable Moloch, who claims everything

© The Author(s) 2020
B. Rojtman, *The Fascination with Death in Contemporary French Thought*, https://doi.org/10.1007/978-3-030-47322-8_8

for himself, it seems we must sacrifice all, even reason—in order, perhaps, to redeem everything. One must give even one's pride, said Bernanos (cf. 1961: 149), retain nothing, for no sanctuary, no guarantee. A celebration of that which is lost, like an offering without name, whose redemptive meaning is forgotten, but which maintains its pathos. Passion without salvation—but charged with the same pain, the same reverence, with the obscure conviction that our destiny is at stake.

The tragic demand does not, therefore, express either resignation or agreement, but rather a disposition to the sublime: the stolid resistance of man, when he faces his ultimate combat, when all the forces come together in him, even those of his disarray and his vanity. There seems to be an intoxication of the extreme that wakes in us the slumbering knight. Our modern sensibility has not broken with this Hegelian Romanticism; it has not forgotten the grandeur of the mortal duel that condemns us to hero-ism. An echo of some ancient chivalric posture, where the essential of man affirms itself in the all-or-nothing of the end. Where the joust is not between peers, but against Nothingness itself, with all that that supposes of intensification and surpassing.

This confrontation has as its first goal the grounding of anthropological difference, man's transcendence over all that is. A dichotomy where his identity is in play, his uniqueness, the exquisiteness of his solitude. The desire for recognition is the desire to be really human, which asserts itself on the threshold of the void, against every biological law. Heir to a long Christian tradition, the hero of modernity bears witness against the visible and turns away from the immediate. The kingdom he aspires to is radically abstract and can be thought of only as elsewhere. A parallel kingdom, autonomous and fabricated, like a 'suprasensible' and disjointed *Nature* which results entirely from 'our free will' (Kant 1997, AK 5:45).

Nothingness now takes an instrumental turn: sole agent of unbinding, sole line of fracture which thought has at its disposal. In order to accede to his humanity, the master seems to seek no other key than that of fear. Death is less terrible, less desolate, than the infamy of being taken by the chill of entropy.

No doubt, these premises explain the all-consuming, necessarily dread-ful character of the test. In order to confirm his strange discordance, man gives the lie to the clay of which he is made, the blood that courses through him. He 'is' only at the cost of no longer living, distancing himself by this mutilation from the encroachment of the mineral. A paradox tied to his hybrid reality, to his rootedness in the terrestrial, to his partaking, despite what he might wish, in the carnal that constitutes him, and which his pride disavows. In order to escape the trap that encloses him, he can only, by means of rebellion, tear at himself all the more, deepen his own wound. He reaches his full stature only at the frontiers of suicide, in the bitterness of the ruin that marks at the same time the only philosophical outcome, the condition of truth, and the abrogation of his quest.

It was this impossible challenge that Hegel made the touchstone of his dialectic. Kojève and his disciples accept the correlate: one must withdraw, one must live despite everything. It is this inverted choice, contrary to the logic of the debate, that prompts new responses. Post-Kojévian writings take their beauty from this foundational aporia, from the detours they find to get around the impasse.

Very early on, under the still strong influence of Kojève's seminar, Bataille proposed a remedy: push the horror of the Nothing back onto existence itself, project its negating power onto immanence. Sacrifice, representation, feast or poetry: so many exit routes, so many ornate substitutes for the traumatism of death. We can see, underlying these various outlets, the same elegance in relation to need, the same disdain for the real and for immediate vicissitudes. In a sort of superior dandyism, Bataille puts a brake on the machine of conditionings; he replaces the transcendence of nothingness with an ideology of the useless. This rupture of purposiveness acts like a little death, an escape *from within* that scatters itself all through a life, disseminating ineffectiveness and dispossession.

True sovereignty thus begins with the absurd, with this 'marvelous wager' (Camus 1991: 46) which leads nowhere, does not demean itself to any calculation of advantage, lets all these false brilliancies fall away. Ontological dignity shows itself in boredom, in a taste for superfluity indifferent to the Good, to all the *common* values, to the stored up riches of body and spirit. Dying to the world accompanies us and frees us, in remembrance of the baroque 'vanities,' where Hebrew hears the word 'breath.'[1] The soul, ever greedy, prefers to be desolate, enlightened by the insignificant, rather than enslaved to the narrow paths of the possible. It finds ease only in disdain. Modern man, subject to no heaven, yet continues to denounce the earth, in the style of the great moralists. To reject that which constrains us, that which reins in our progress toward the absent star, whose dawning appears beyond the desolation.

---

[1] The biblical word *hevel* means first of all *breath*, and then metaphorically the vanity of all things (cf. *Ecclesiastes* 1:1). It is also the Hebrew name of Abel, fated, as if by his essence, to die.

This disinterest, in an echo of Hegel, overlaps with a profoundly humanist and estranging concern. It is still the same faculty of phantasm and ideal, but now centered on inaction, thirsting for indolence. It limits itself to mesmerization, content only to die, slowly—letting go little by little of its treasures, casting off all realization, all progress, all recompense—which is also to say, letting go of all fallacious compensation, in the name of a declared and constant coolness, of sterile gestures that turn into representation. This need for passivity, for relinquishment, this philosophical and poetic breakdown, throws overboard the impedimenta of existing. In order to go straight to the heart of what humanity means, in the reduction of ourselves to ourselves, the knapsack empty. I am the knight of darkness. At the end of all functionality, all utility, what remains when action is worn out, when it becomes only spectacle. I am he who is. With no other role than that of renunciation. Without act, without intention, bar that of being perceived. The *potlatch* is a rite of passage—from having to being, from event to presence; it is visualization and sacrament.

From Kojève to Lacan, this bravado in the style of Hugo's Gavroche raises us up to beauty: which *serves* for nothing, takes its meaning from no external objective. A desire frozen into myth, as unsubstantial as the image, strengthened by its own impotence; it sums up in itself the formidableness and strangeness of being, the pain of existing for no reason. From atop his abdication, the hero of nothingness has nothing to pursue or to deserve any more; he lets himself be seen, only, finally, for what he is: man.

This heroism of *weakness*[2] confounds at the same time the constructions of the spirit: the fallacious conquests of metaphysics, the consoling precision of reason—everything which, in human civilization, has sought to tame the elements, to reduce the random or give it meaning. For the successors of Kojève, achievement and truth are themselves relegated to the rank of 'goods': so many mediocre values, shrunken to the scale of the system. The exactitude of the rule and the circularity of phenomena, be they scientific or metaphysical, transcendent or immanent, are all part of the same Enemy, all present the same impersonal and certain face: a flawless constancy, an endless servitude. From the uniform seed of matter to the invariability of the Law, it is the same prison that has to be torn down.

---

[2] 'Observing all this and much more of a like nature, one might well wonder whether the only possible heroism was the heroism of the weak. Yet what heroism was more at one with the times?' (Mann 2005: 17).

No asperity. No otherwise, for the madness of being to rush into, no void through which to become, in which to catch one's breath. The metaphysics of the One is now nothing but the transposed form of inescapable nature, where consciousness suffocates.

Man is thus what nothing, not even the absolute, can contain. Too narrow for his unhappiness, the plenitude that encircles him impoverishes him and limits him to the universal. It is in the face of this totalitarian indigence that the postulation is put in place that is inherent to our contemporary culture, that of liberty. Not the anarchic liberty of *everything is permitted*, but a fluidity of principle, a region of metamorphosis and of indetermination, whose horizon Heidegger, more than anyone else, has opened up for us; for man, there is no fixed destiny, nothing that vitiates his contingency. Death, rather, is the sign of his marvelous undecidability—of his wavering, of his perpetual dehiscence. An amalgam of the infinitely open and the tomb, where the contemporary tragedy is enacted. Death appears here as the condition and the accomplice of a *disorientation*, of an unbounded surge that turns only toward death itself. Death as companion, that alone unfurls before us the vast ether of infinities, a protean becoming, for which there is no program. Something is continually rolling on under the banner of death, moving and starting anew, some plasticity to be maintained, some fundamental and subtle indefiniteness, more aerial than anything living. The ethics of Levinas foresaw it, in refusing to have the morality of man depend on his persistence. Permanence is his damnation; homogeneity a fetter. Against all that recalls the Parmenidean immutable, contrary to all identity, to all concordance, postmodern lyricism fervently defends a vow of excess and of slippage which puts man back into his turmoil, always thrown, overflowing, as if borne on some torrent that no dam can hold. With its fluctuating norms, its blurred edges and its approximations, this stream overturns metaphysical rigidity in order to return to some earlier memory, of a prior chaos and a molten earth.

How can one tell now if there is only one path, only this pallid rage, to ground disobedience to the Rule, and to ensure the impetuosity of this outburst? If the face of the absolute can only be *metaphysical*, can only offer itself to human need in this—asphyxiated—form of perfection? Must we denounce all truth in order to blaze ahead, to breathlessly maintain the momentum that pushes us on? Must we, in the name of our historicity, burn all the signs, all that in life stops us and tempts us, all that orients us and fulfills us? In the name of some inexhaustible despair, are we to invent a solely negating future? For the purposes of what vain quest, whose only reason or refuge is itself, are we to carry out a project only if it is destroyed from the outset, and an action only if it is forged in smoke? That which trembles in disquiet in our civilization, in estrangement from the world, will it not find any epiphany but death, any remedy but this step into the darkness, this dissolution at every instant, drawn by the silence of the grave? Where is one now to find the breaking of that embrace, by what *otherwise*? Is there no other way but unhappiness—which would, nonetheless, give us back to the fluidity of space, to the levity of the inexistent, in the insubstantial mist of sky blue?

With the last great texts of subversion, the absolute itself seems to join the dance, to start to turn. The dismantled absolute, subverted from within, that melts in its turn, like Dali's watches. By virtue of no longer being, the Idea itself seems to move by degrees, and in its turn yields and splits. To deconstruct is to reinvent the unnumberable. A web without end, that breathes and changes, such is the merry vertigo of the new philosophy, whose dream is movement. A vision of a sun that has fallen, a whole sky of harmony and spheres that is coming apart. But while eternity totters, while the Unanimous dissolves, on the ontological horizon the Nothing is ever rising, purer, more enchanting and disembodied, spreading through the void. Death is, again, the name of this fall, absolutely without marker, of this more tormented hope, of this truth corroded by absence, in which the current generation finds its idol. In the post-modern allegory, the vessels are continually breaking. The world is great and lies waste, and shakes its debris like a bird its wings, in the name of a more formless prior state where consciousness knows itself.

This lacunary ideal cannot be faced directly. It no longer has the granitic splendor of Night. To the solitary knight, it no longer promises any tragic halo, no sudden overcoming. Its ashen pallor requires a lateral approach, more patient, more hushed, the effort of a long-term undermining. The soul's detachment is no longer an event but a condition, a lost country, a diaphaneity of the air, which evaporates infinitely. Death as a reverse side, a modality, an environment and not the instant. One must survive, as if this were to finally die, between nature and nothingness; one must endlessly maintain the dazzled shock of slipping under. For this moment is no longer panic, no longer has the sharpness of a climax. Rather, it brings experience back to this side of the frontier: that which cannot be brought to closure, that which announces the wandering of the Straight Line. To live without crossing the limit, between chasm and earth, to stick to the interstice, in order to better disorient the Law. Without fighting it, going around it, sidestepping it in this gentler style which is that of whiteness. Blanchot bleaches, Derrida dodges or displaces, both equally elude the grasp of the Logos, revealing lands lying fallow at the margins of totality. Fields untilled, labyrinths of wild grasses. They show us an elsewhere, the clear-sightedness of disaster, the necessity of not being—but in a different way from that of the master or the knight: no longer in the glorious dust of peril, but rather in a play of will-o-the-wisps that leads astray, and scatters the pain of existing over the surface of the years.

It is at this point of destructuration that the Jewish Kabbalah enters the scene: it takes up the task of these slippages, these vaguenesses, follows their disappointments, enters the ballet of the intangible. The Kabbalah with its sinuous forms, which responds to the contemporary imaginary through its nebulous metaphysics, its fragmentary and pulsating version of the divine. It describes the same kind of drift as the contemporary imaginary's, its trails of shooting stars, the same succession of waterfalls. Its orientation unites everything that is incessant and liquid in the Heraclitean proposition. But if it espouses this back and forth, it is in order to better reveal the essentiality of these vibrations, of these trajectories, in order to better vivify their dispersal, the better to pour into these accidents the alchemy of its light.

For the desire of death, we now understand, is not its own end in itself: it is only the circuitous, as if bashful, expression of a desire to live—but so poignant that none of life's luster can dull it. An expectation of something which would be greater than oneself, and which no wisdom assuages, no narrow or credulous distraction. The great suffering that racks humanity cannot be corrupted by the mirages of immortality. Its fierce contestation can never cease, nor its insistence, stronger than the universe that kills us, on bearing witness in the name of something irrepressible, within us, that continues to cry out.

Death is only an *ersatz*. A window out of the anxiety of being, out of the frantic protestation of humanity. I hear, under the bitter indictment of the moderns, under this desolate dandyism, a long hunger to live. But without ties, like the great migrators, as it should have been. A postulation of liberty that grows so vexed as to refuse and reject the false assurances, the cowardly indulgences. Which turns its back on the Idea—in the name of a more violent dream, at the cliff edge. An inverse desire that can be expressed only through aversion, an impatience to be, thrown on some

Herculean pyre, burning from still wanting. Living as if from the reverse side, with negation, a patrician sarcasm, as man's sole resort. The post-modern denounces, takes flight on velvet wings, into an untenable sky, that says 'death, death,' the better to celebrate, to bear away the last of the dross, never sparing of itself, counting as nothing the mourning of that which is. In the name of this sensed majesty, common to the human species, of this solemn shadowed side of the mountain, that is only glimpsed by dint of its darkness. To at least die, if nothing is granted us, as close as we can to the unbearable. For nothingness carries us toward the lands of intoxication, nothingness as sole key to a truth in fragments, to a beyond that is more arid, more ravine-strewn and more human, that all the blandnesses of utopia.

I hear the grandeur of these collapses, these haughty and destructive rites. I hear the escape of Eros, his Icarian flight, his precipice joy—where nothing mires him any more, this vast plateau where his destitution vaults high, free, and burned to bits.

Yet, we must live. We must take with us the shore's defeat, the foggy beaches, where fade into the distance the galloping hooves. What death gives us, life proclaims in its evanescence, through the mirages of morning. Bottomless life, shaded with phantoms, lined with veins, intersections, ruptures. Immaterial life, sinuous and exposed, its frail promise of serene chasms.

The prize for the human is not of his own being, is not won from disaster. He does not go unto death as one sets out upon the open sea. His life alone is already wind, swirling with sparks, while he ruins himself in existing. His life alone is enough, already resembles the infinite, through the vertigo that accompanies it, and carries with it endless fissures. And in this endless fall in the country of sand, he opens barriers, forces his way on carmine worlds, then gives himself up to the light, in the subtle vapor of the unfinished.

BIBLIOGRAPHY

Bataille, Georges. 2012. *Literature and Evil*. Trans. A. Hamilton. London: Penguin.
Bernanos, Georges. 1961. *Journal d'un curé de campagne*. Paris: Le Livre de Poche.
Camus, Albert. 1991. *The Myth of Sisyphus*. Trans. J. O'Brien. London: Penguin.
Kant, Emmanuel. 1997. *The Critique of Practical Reason*. Trans. M.J. Gregor. Cambridge: Cambridge University Press.
Mann, Thomas. 2005. *Death in Venice*. Trans. M.H. Heim. London: Harper Collins.

BIBLIOGRAPHY

Abel, Olivier. 2007. *Paul Ricœur: Vivant jusqu'à la mort*. Paris: Seuil.

Alter, Yehuda Arieh Leib. 1872/2000. *Sefat Emet*. Merkaz Shapira: Yeshivat Or Etsion.

Aristotle. 2011. *Nicomachean Ethics*. Trans. R.C. Bartlett and S.D. Collins. Chicago: The University of Chicago Press.

Askénazi, Léon. 1987. *Le 7 Adar (anniversaire de Moïse) et la fête de Pourim*. Lecture at Yaïr Center, Jerusalem.

———. 1973. La notion de sainteté dans la pensée du Rav Kook. Twelfth Conference of French-Language Jewish Intellectuals: The Jews in a Desacralized Society, 31 October 1971. In *L'Autre dans la conscience juive, le sacré et le couple*, ed. J. Halpérin and G. Lévitte, 80–100. Paris: Presses Universitaires de France.

Atlan, Henri. 1979. *Entre le cristal et la fumée: Essai sur l'organisation du vivant*. Paris: Seuil.

Auffret, Dominique. 1990. *Alexandre Kojève: La philosophie, l'État, la fin de l'Histoire*. Paris: Grasset et Fasquelle.

Bataille, Georges. 1962. *Death and Sensuality: A Study of Eroticism and the Taboo*. Trans. M. Dalwood. New York: Walker and Company.

———. 1973. *L'expérience intérieure*. Paris: Gallimard.

———. 1985. The Practice of Joy in the Face of Death. In *Visions of Excess: Selected Writings, 1927–1939*, trans. A. Stoekl, 235–239. Minneapolis: University of Minnesota Press.

———. 1988a. *Inner Experience*. Trans. L.A. Boldt. New York: SUNY Press.

———. 1988b. *The Accursed Share: An Essay on General Economy*. Trans. R. Hurley. New York: Zone Books.

———. 1988c. *Guilty*. Trans. B. Boone. Venice Beach, CA: Lapis.

© The Author(s) 2020   133
B. Rojtman, *The Fascination with Death in Contemporary French Thought*, https://doi.org/10.1007/978-3-030-47322-8

————. 1997a. Hegel, Death and Sacrifice. Trans. J. Strauss. In *The Bataille Reader*, ed. F. Botting and S. Wilson, 279–295. London: Blackwell.

————. 1997b. Knowledge of Sovereignty. In *The Bataille Reader*, ed. F. Botting and S. Wilson, 301–312. London: Blackwell.

————. 1997c. Schema of Sovereignty. In *The Bataille Reader*, ed. F. Botting and S. Wilson, 313–320. London: Blackwell.

————. 1997d. Letter to X, Lecturer on Hegel. In *The Bataille Reader*, ed. F. Botting and S. Wilson, 296–300. London: Blackwell.

————. 2001. Method of Meditation. In *The Unfinished System of Nonknowledge*, 77–99. Minneapolis: University of Minnesota Press.

————. 2012. *Literature and Evil*. Trans. A. Hamilton. London: Penguin.

Beaufret, Jean. 2013. *Parménide, le Poème*. Paris: Presses Universitaires de France.

Bergson, Henri. 1946. *The Creative Mind*. Trans. M.L. Andison. New York: Philosophical Library.

Bernanos, Georges. 1961. *Journal d'un curé de campagne*. Paris: Le Livre de Poche.

Beuman, Shaul. 1937/1977. *Sefer Maphte'hei 'Hokhmat Haemet*. Jerusalem: No publisher.

Blanchot, Maurice. 1982. *The Space of Literature*. Trans. A. Smock. Lincoln: University of Nebraska Press.

————. 1993. *The Infinite Conversation*. Trans. S. Hanson. Minneapolis and London: University of Minnesota Press.

Bonnefoy, Yves. 1983. *L'Improbable et autres essais*. Paris: Gallimard.

Borges, Jorge Luis. 1998. The Secret Miracle. In *Collected Fictions*, trans. A. Hurley, 82–85. London: Penguin.

Butler, Judith. 1987. *Subjects of Desire: Hegelian Reflections in Twentieth-Century France*. New York: Columbia University Press.

Camus, Albert. 1991. *The Myth of Sisyphus*. Trans. J. O'Brien. London: Penguin.

Dastur, Françoise. 1996. *Death: An Essay on Finitude*. Trans. J. Llewelyn. London and Atlantic Highlands, NJ: Athlone.

Derrida, Jacques. 1982. *Margins of Philosophy*. Trans. A. Bass. Brighton: Harvester Press.

————. 1986. *Glas*. Trans. J.P. Leavy and R. Rand. Lincoln: University of Nebraska Press.

————. 1989. *Memoirs for Paul de Man, Revised Edition*. Trans. C. Lindsay, J. Culler, E. Cadava, and P. Kamuf. New York: Columbia University Press.

————. 2001. From Restricted to General Economy: A Hegelianism without Reserve. In *Writing and Difference*, trans. Alan Bass, 317–350. London: Routledge.

Descombes, Vincent. 1979. *Le Même et l'Autre: quarante-cinq ans de philosophie française (1933–1978)*. Paris: Minuit.

Epstein, Ye'hiel Michel Halevi. 1905/2006. *Arukh Hashul'han, Ora'h 'Hayim*. No Publisher.

Fénelon, François. 1972. *Correspondance*. Éd. Jean Orcibal. Paris: Klincksieck.

———. 1983a. Lettres et Opuscules spirituels XXIII. In *Œuvres I*, ed. Jacques Le Brun. Paris: Gallimard.

———. 1983b. Explication des maximes des saints sur la vie intérieure. In *Œuvres* t. 1, ed. J. Le Brun. Paris: Gallimard.

Filoni, Marco. 2010. *Le Philosophe du dimanche. La vie et la pensée d'Alexandre Kojève*. Trans. G. Larché. Paris: Gallimard.

Freud, Sigmund. 1895/1950. Project for a New Scientific Psychology. In *The Standard Edition* 1, 281–397. London: Hogarth Press.

———. 1915/1957. Instincts and Their Vicissitudes. Trans. J. Strachey. In *Standard Edition* 14, 117–140. London: Hogarth Press.

———. 1920/1961. *Beyond the Pleasure Principle*. Trans. J. Strachey. New York: WW Norton.

———. 1925/1961. Negation. Trans. J. Strachey. In *Standard Edition* 19, 235–239. London: Hogarth Press.

———. 1930/1961. *Civilization and Its Discontents*. Trans. J. Riviere. London: Hogarth Press.

———. 1930/2000. *Le Malaise dans la culture*. Trans. J. André. Paris: Presses Universitaires de France.

Guyomard, Patrick. 1992. *La Jouissance du tragique: Antigone, Lacan et le désir de l'analyste*. Paris: Aubier.

Hacohen, Zadok. 1922/1972. *Peri Zadik*, T. III, *Vayikra, Emor*. Jerusalem: Books Export Enterprises.

Haver, Yits'hak Isaac. n.d. (Orig. publ. Warsaw, 1888). *Pit'hei Shearim*. Ed. M. Kessin. Tel-Aviv: Brazni.

Hegel, G.W.F. 1913. *Jenaer Realphilosophie I: Die Vorlesungen von 1803/4*. Leipzig: Hoffmeister.

———. 1966. *Phénoménologie de l'Esprit*. Trans. J. Hyppolite. Paris: Aubier-Montaigne.

———. 1975. *Lectures on the Philosophy of World History: Introduction: Reason in History*. Trans. H.B. Nisbet. Cambridge: Cambridge University Press.

———. 1979. *System of Ethical Life and First Philosophy of Spirit*. Trans. H.S. Harris and T.M. Knox. New York: SUNY Press.

———. 1991. *Elements of the Philosophy of Right*. Trans. H.B. Nisbet. Cambridge: Cambridge University Press.

———. 2018. *The Phenomenology of Spirit*. Trans. M. Inwood. Oxford: Oxford University Press.

Heidegger, Martin. 1990. *Questions III et IV*. Paris: Gallimard.

———. 1996. *Being and Time*. Trans. J. Stambaugh. New York: SUNY Press.

———. 2001. The Thing. In *Poetry, Language Thought*, trans. M. Hofstadter, 163–180. New York: Harper.

Hobbes, Thomas. 1949. *De Cive or The Citizen*. Ed. P. Lamprecht. New York: Appleton-Century-Crofts.

———. 1994. *Leviathan*. Ed. E. Curley. Indianapolis and Cambridge: Hackett.

———. 2008. *The Elements of Law, Natural and Politic*. Ed. J.C.A. Gaskin. Oxford and New York: Oxford University Press.

Hollier, Denis. 1995. *Le Collège de Sociologie, 1937–1939*. Paris: Gallimard.

Jackson, John E. 1982. *La Mort Baudelaire: Essai sur les Fleurs du Mal*. Neuchâtel: La Baconnière.

Jankélévitch, Vladimir. 2011. *L'Irréversible et la nostalgie*. Paris: Flammarion.

Jarczyk, Gwendoline, and Pierre-Jean Labarrière. 1996. *De Kojève à Hegel: Cent cinquante ans de pensée hégélienne en France*. Paris: Albin Michel.

Kant, Emmanuel. 1996. *Groundwork of the Metaphysics of Morals*. Trans. M.J. Gregor. In *Practical Philosophy*. Cambridge: Cambridge University Press.

———. 1997. *The Critique of Practical Reason*. Trans. M.J. Gregor. Cambridge: Cambridge University Press.

Kojève, Alexandre. 1969. *Introduction to the Reading of Hegel: Lectures on the Phenomenology of Spirit*. Ed. R. Queneau and A. Bloom, trans. J.H. Nichols. Ithaca and London: Cornell University Press.

———. 1973. The Idea of Death in the Philosophy of Hegel: (Complete Text of the Last Two Lectures of the Academic Year 1933–34). Trans. J.J. Carpino. *Interpretation* 3/2,3, 114–156.

———. 1993. Note inédite sur Hegel et Heidegger. In *Rue Descartes* no. 7, 39.

———. 1997. *Introduction à la lecture de Hegel: Leçons sur la* Phénoménologie de l'Esprit. Ed. R. Queneau. Paris: Gallimard.

———. 1998. *L'Athéisme*. Trans. N. Ivanoff and L. Bibard. Paris: Gallimard.

Kook, Avraham Yits'hak Hacohen. 1888/1985. *Orot Hakodesh* 2nd Part, Vol. 3 *Mussar Hakodesh*. Ed. D. Cohen. Jerusalem: Mossad Harav Kook.

Koyré, Alexandre. 1971. Hegel à Iéna. In *Études d'histoire de la pensée philosophique*. Paris: Gallimard.

Kristeva, Julia. 1987. *Black Sun: Depression and Melancholy*. Trans. L.S. Roudiez. New York: Columbia University Press.

Lacan, Jacques. 1986. *Le Séminaire de Jacques Lacan: Livre Vii: L'éthique De La Psychanalyse 1959–1960*. Ed. J-A. Miller. Paris: Seuil.

———. 1992. *The Seminar: Book VII: The Ethics of Psychoanalysis 1959–1960*. Ed. J-A. Miller and trans. D. Porter. New York: WW Norton.

———. 2001. *Écrits: A Selection*. Trans. A. Sheridan. London: Routledge.

Laplanche, J., and J.B. Pontalis. 1973. *The Language of Psycho-Analysis*. Trans. D. Nicholson-Smith. London: The Hogarth Press.

Le Brun, Jacques. 2002. *Le Pur Amour de Platon à Lacan*. Paris: Seuil.

Levinas, Emmanuel. 1979. *Totality and Infinity: An Essay on Exteriority*. Trans. A. Lingis. The Hague: Martinus Nijhoff.

———. 1985. *Ethics and Infinity: Conversations with Philippe Nemo*. Trans. R.A. Cohen. Pittsburgh: Duquesne University Press.

———. 1987. *Time and the Other, and Additional Essays*. Trans. R.A. Cohen. Pittsburgh: Duquesne University Press.

———. 1988. *Existence and Existents*. Trans. A. Lingis. Dordrecht: Kluwer.

———. 2004. *De l'existence à l'existant*. Paris: Vrin.

Loew ben Bezalel, Yehuda. 1589/1971. *Derekh ha'Hayim*. Bnei Brak: Yahadut.

Maimonides. 2006. *Séfer Hamitzvot (Book of Commandments)*. Trans. B. Bell. New York: Sichos.

Mann, Thomas. 2005. *Death in Venice*. Trans. M.H. Heim. London: HarperCollins.

Marquet, Jean-François. 2009. *Leçons sur la Phénoménologie de l'esprit de Hegel*. Paris: Ellipses.

Nancy, Jean-Luc. 1991. *The Inoperative Community*. Ed. P. Connor and trans. P. Connor, L. Garbus, M. Holland, and S. Sawhney. Minneapolis and Oxford: University of Minnesota Press.

———. 1997. *The Sense of the World*. Trans. J.S. Librett. Minneapolis: University of Minnesota Press.

———. 2002. *Hegel: The Restlessness of the Negative*. Trans. J. Smith and S. Miller. Minneapolis: University of Minnesota Press.

Nietzsche, Friedrich. 1969. *Thus Spoke Zarathustra: A Book for Everyone and No-One*. Trans. R.J. Hollingdale. London: Penguin.

Nietzsche, Frederick. 1999. *The Birth of Tragedy and Other Writings*. Trans. R. Speirs. Cambridge: Cambridge University Press.

Nietzsche, Friedrich. 2001. *The Gay Science*. Ed. B. Williams and trans. J. Nauckhoff and A. Del Caro. Cambridge: Cambridge University Press.

Plato. 1981. *Phaedo*. In *Five Dialogues*, trans. G.M.A. Grube. Indianapolis: Hackett.

Revault d'Allonnes, Myriam. 2006. Cet Éros par quoi nous sommes dans l'Être. *Esprit* 3: 276–289.

Ricœur, Paul. 1974. *Conflict of Interpretations*. Ed. D. Ihde. Northwestern University Press.

———. 2009/1960. *Finitude et culpabilité*. Paris: Aubier.

Rojtman, Betty. 1991. *Une grave distraction*. Paris: Balland.

Schopenhauer, Arthur. 2010. *The World as Will and Representation*. Trans. and ed. J. Norman et al. Cambridge: Cambridge University Press.

Sichère, Bernard. 2006. Bataille et les fascistes. In *Pour Bataille: être, chance, souveraineté*. Paris: Gallimard.

Steiner, George. 1996. *Antigones: How the Antigone Legend Has Endured in Western Literature, Art, and Thought*. Yale: Yale University Press.

Sterlitz, Shimeon. 1966. Hatsehuva leor histakluto shel rabenu. Appendix to Abraham Isaac Hacohen Kook, *Orot Hateshuva*. Merkaz Shapira: Yeshivat Or Etsion.

Strauss, Leo. 1952. *The Political Philosophy of Hobbes: Its Basis and Its Genesis.* Trans. E.M. Sinclair. Chicago: University of Chicago Press.

Surya, Georges. 1992. *Georges Bataille: la mort à l'œuvre.* Paris: Gallimard.

Vigée, Claude. 1960. *Les Artistes de la faim.* Paris: Calmann-Lévy.

Zarader, Marlène. 2001. *L'Être et le neutre: A partir de Maurice Blanchot.* Paris: Verdier.

———. 2006. *The Unthought Debt: Heideger and the Hebraic Heritage.* Trans. B. Bergo. Stanford: Stanford University Press.

INDEX[1]

[1] Note: Page numbers followed by 'n' refer to notes.

© The Author(s) 2020
B. Rojtman, *The Fascination with Death in Contemporary French Thought*, https://doi.org/10.1007/978-3-030-47322-8

CPSIA information can be obtained
at www.ICGtesting.com
Printed in the USA
LVHW050401291220
675234LV00009B/615

9 783030 473211